journey
into My Brother's Soul

journey
into My Brother's Soul

Maria D. Dowd

JOURNEY INTO MY BROTHER'S SOUL

A New Spirit Novel

ISBN-13: 978-0-373-83029-9
ISBN-10:   0-373-83029-7

www.kimanipress.com

Printed in U.S.A.

Acknowledgments

This book is dedicated to my beloved husband, Curtis V, the man who picked me out of a crowd, and *knew* that this happy-nappy head would be his...for life. We met on a cruise to Aruba during the summer of 2005 and fell in love on the back of a Jet Ski, with me holding on for dear life. We are imperfectly perfect mates, best friends and soul sources for what feeds our spirits, minds and bodies. I'm eternally thankful to God for bringing us into each other's lives...on the ship's lido deck, in the middle of the Atlantic Ocean...terribly apropos for a man who so loves the sea. I love you. I love you, Curtis V.

This book is also dedicated to my stepdaddy— Richard Mordecai Washington Sr.—who reared me from the age of nine, and was everything but a "step" in my life. He taught me how to "suck it up" and take it like a man, in our perpetually losing games of penny poker. And, he was relentless about daily reading time. As a result, I inhaled novels, and so vividly remember my first book about black folks, *Daddy Was a Numbers Runner.* I've been on that track ever since. While Dad's required reading hour was a no-brainer for me, that nine-o'clock bedtime on school nights, at the ripe old age of thirteen, was a bit much...so I thought *then.*

Much love to my brothers, Arron, William, Tarik and Richard; my new son-friends, Mann (the cowboy, like his dad) and Quebec (the musician, like his dad); and my African-American Women on Tour brothers, Norvell and Sylvester, who, during our thirteen-year conference tour stint, lived by the motto "Anything for Maria." Your steadfast friendship has been priceless. Every memory brings about a smile. And, big hugs to my uncles Willie (my mother's alter ego) and Kenneth, who inspired my entrepreneurial spirit.

Finally, a special tribute to my beloved grandfather who transitioned some years back. The evidence of his godliness, belief in higher education and no-nonsense, disciplined living continues to radiate light into every corner of my existence. Although I couldn't bring myself ever to hook that pension-paying civil-service job (too much Uncle Ken in me for that!), I can stand tall in his Heavenly Glow. Speaking for my entire family, thank you, Grandfather, for doing what needed to be done to fill Grandmother's last years with love, comfort and grace.

JOURNEY TO COMMUNITY EMPOWERMENT

LOVE NOTES

JOURNEY INTO MY SOUL

Etta sings "Teach Me"
I catch your scent in the air
Hear life's true meaning

—Reginald Lockett

Dedication To Care for My Soul

BY WILLIAM B. T. TAYLOR

This moment I dedicate my life

to the care of my soul.

To the care of my home,

my body, my surroundings.

Care for what I put into my body

and what comes out of my mouth.

I now choose to listen

to my soul, moment to moment.

I dedicate my life to doing what my soul tells me to do,

no matter what, no matter how hard or odd.

Even if the task seems impossible

or undesirable, I will trust my soul.

I will follow its dictates.

I know when my soul calls,

the hunches, the visions,

the still small voice,

even the loud inner scream.

My soul has called many times before,

but I did not always listen.

I did not always follow.

Now I will, in all ways follow.

I dedicate my life to following my soul, my dreams.

Following the infinite possibilities within me.

I dedicate my life to the care of my soul.

For my soul is the voice and the life of God.

Here I Stand

BY T. S. MURPHY

Here I Stand

Since the dawn of time

The dusk of days gone by

I am a product of

The clay of fertile Ethiopian ground,

The Middle Passage,

The rebellion in the cotton fields,

The renaissance of our souls,

The revolution of our strengths,

The revelation of our spirits,

The evolution of a seed

From a woman warrior

Here I Stand

Bearing witness to

The good and bad, night and day, birth and death

I am one in many and in many I am one

With you, the world, the universe,

I am a part of divine order

All that I have been through, have learned, will go through

Will shape me and my tribulations to come

Being that Faith is the substance of things hoped for,

The evidence of things not seen

Who is man to question my existence

I am because I believe I am

Here I Stand

Before you

Humble and proud /African and American

Body tired and soul strong

But above all else

I Stand

Like the strong men before me

And those yet to come

There Is No Death—Over There

BY TY GRAY-EL

I was born with scarlet fever. Back in the '50s, scientists still had not gotten a grip on the disease and lots of people died. My mother and father had two sons before me. They are buried over in Arlington Cemetery because my dad was in the army at the time. Neither of them lived beyond six months of age. I, too, was born with the fatal disease and was not expected to survive past my sixth month. I did, but for the first seven years of my life, I suffered periodic fevers.

Forty-plus years later, of all the memories I have, one is most vivid. In my seventh year, I was stricken with fever so terribly that my mother called an ambulance, terrified that she was about to lose her third and only surviving son to this dreaded disease. I recall her bending over me with an ice-filled washcloth and applying it to my forehead in an attempt to keep me cool. She was crying. I recall those next few moments as if they were yesterday. I can vividly remember leaving my body on a thin white thread that looked like a translucent umbilical cord. I floated up to the ceiling in the living room of the one-bedroom tenement walk-up we lived in, in northeast Washington, D.C. I rose from my body as mist would rise on a foggy break of day.

When I got to the ceiling, I looked over at what is still the most beautiful sight I have ever seen. I remember hues of bright, sky-like blues and magnificent gold. I could see a light that was electric, yet completely indescribable. It was pleasant and serene. I was awed and humbled. I recall my chest catching my breath. I remember smiling as I looked down at myself lying on the green hideaway couch that served as my bed. I looked at my mother's tears running down her cheeks as she agonized over the thought of losing me.

I said to her, "Ma, stop crying. You're going before I go and there's nothing to cry about. It's beautiful over here." I can still see the way she looked up at the spot where my soul seemed to hover. She had this quizzical look on her face I'll never forget, as if she heard something but was not quite sure what it was. Then, I looked back at paradise. That's the closest word I can find to describe what I saw. Paradise.

In that instant, I came to realize that there is no death.

Instead, there is existence after this earthly experience. I have proof, intangible proof within my heart and my soul. My proof lies in the very thoughts I am transferring to this paper. Yet, I cannot grasp these words physically, anymore than I can grip my soul. I had the pleasure of visiting beyond, of transcending my flesh. I am totally convinced that life continues after what we perceive as death. In fact, I believe there is no death. Nothing dies, just transforms.

Images

BY JAMES E. CHERRY

Even after the preacher mumbled a few dry words: "ashes

to ashes and dust to dust…" and they bestowed your body

back to earth, your presence hovered over my shoulder,

timeless sculptures on the shelf of my life.

Chiseled cheekbones, classic lines, eyes deep-set prophetic

   oracles, the glory of antiquity, the beauty

of shadows, profiles in sculpted ebony where I catch

my own imperfections, shortcomings, possibilities.

I am of the same clay the potter chose.

The War Within the War

BY RONALD HARRIS

"We are now over the Republic of Vietnam and will be landing in approximately ten minutes. Please observe the No Smoking sign and fasten your seat belts. May God be with you all."

As the plane descended at Tan Son Nhut Airport in Saigon on an exceedingly humid evening, reality began to seep in. I was finally here. Ever since receiving my military orders Thanksgiving Eve assigning me to the Republic of Vietnam, I had endeavored to prepare myself for this very moment. As the plane made its final approach and the No Smoking and Fasten Your Seat Belts signs flashed off, I pondered what destiny had planned for me and whether or not I had made the right decision when I enlisted only a week after graduating from high school.

Coming from a family of seven children, whose parents were both deceased, I was raised by my grandmother. A woman with only a fourth-grade education, my grandmother always stressed the importance of obtaining a high-school diploma. In fact, she was emphatic when it came to education.

"Being colored and uneducated is a curse," she often preached.

If I had heard it once I had heard it a thousand times. Before my last year of high school, I'd been a pretty good student, even making the honor roll a few times, which made Grandma proud. However, during the last semester of my senior year, I began to cut classes and hang in the streets. I passed, *barely*. In fact, on the day we were to receive our final report cards I was so fearful that I'd flunked English, I had my friend Nat pick up my report card. When he told me I had gotten a D, I did cartwheels all the way home.

Fifteen minutes after landing we arrived at the already crowded USO. There were twelve occupied telephone booths with a short line of GIs waiting impatiently outside each. There were four men ahead of me, and calls were lasting about thirty minutes each. The wait was killing me. To suppress my anxiety, I began studying the facial expressions of everyone in my line before and after using the phone. The distinction was like night and day. Frowns were turned upside down as everyone wiped away tears of happiness or sighed with great relief. As I entered the booth and sat, my knees shivered uncontrollably. I called Grandma first. As the operator made the connections, it occurred to me that this was the first time I could recall ever telephoning her. I just knew she'd think something was wrong. She had written me a letter and I needed to hear her voice.

The phone rang six times before she answered, faintly.

"Hello? Who is it?"

"Mom, it's me, Tommy, your grandson!"

"Tommy?! Oh God, Tommy!! Is this really you? What's wrong? You all right? Why are you calling so late?" I had forgotten about the thirteen-hour time difference. It was 1:35 on a Sunday morning where she lived.

"Yeah, Mom, everything is just fine. Your letter kinda bothered me a bit and I just wanted to call and make sure everything's okay."

I heard a sniffle in the background.

"Don't cry, Mom. Really, everything's fine."

After she reassured me that nothing was amiss, I told her I was sorry for calling so late.

"Well, Mom, it's late so I'll let you go back to sleep. I know you have to get up early for church. I love you."

"I love you too, baby. Take good care of yourself. Are you reading your Bible?"

"Yes, ma'am."

"Well, I want you to read Saint Mark 8:38, okay?"

"Okay."

"And always remember—"

"Yeah, I know," I interrupted. "Jesus loves me and so do you."

"That's right, baby! Take good care of yourself."

After hanging up the phone, I realized that although I loved my grandmother more than anyone in the world, this was the first time I could recall telling her.

Because I had been in Vietnam more than one hundred and twenty days, I was granted R&R to Hawaii. On the day prior to my departure, I received an unexpected letter from my aunt Edith. When I opened it, a small leaflet fell to the floor. When I picked it up and unfolded it, I went numb. It was an obituary with a picture of Grandma on the front! My knees buckled and I begin sobbing uncontrollably.

"Oh nooooo! Oh nooooo! It can't be! Please God, say it ain't so!" I wept uncontrollably. The next thing I knew, a fellow solider was standing over me with a cold, wet towel in his hand. I had fainted. Grandma died of a stroke only one week after I had telephoned her.

I canceled my R&R the next day, opting instead to take a weekend pass to Vung Tau, a seaport resort not far from Long Binh. I needed solitude. For two days, I just lay on the beach trying to imagine how life would be without Grandma. She had been the finest human being who ever lived. How could God be so cruel? Then I recalled something she told me after my mother's funeral.

"God has a plan for each of us," she said. "Everything He does, no matter how cruel it may seem, has a purpose. Do not question His motives."

What plans could He have by taking you from me? I asked myself. She loved Him so, and this was her reward?

At that moment, I had an apparition. Grandma appeared in our living room, clad in her flowered housedress, rocking in her favorite chair. She was talking to God.

Lord, I've served you faithfully with devotion for seventy years and not once have I asked you for anything for myself. But now my precious baby is in Vietnam fighting an evil war. You know his heart, Lord, and that he's a good boy. Please watch over him. She was weeping. Startled, I leaped to my feet just as a cold chill swept across my body. I smelled the scent of her favorite perfume. I wept again and again.

The Cream Shall Rise

BY TY GRAY-EL

When I was seven years old, my grandmother taught me one of the most empowering lessons I've ever learned. In the late 1950s and early 60s, the milkman would deliver milk to houses in glass quart bottles. He would wear a white hat, a white uniform, white shoes and drive a white milk truck. He'd always deliver early in the morning, usually before most people got up. One spring morning, Grandma told me to bring the milk in. I handed it to her and she set it on the kitchen table, then made me sit down in front of it and look closely at the bottle. She asked me what I saw. I said, "I see milk, Grandma, that's all I see." She made me sit there and stare at that bottle of milk for more than five minutes. Again she asked, "What do you see?"

Now, as you might imagine, I was a frustrated little seven-year-old boy who thought his grandmother was trippin' because all I could see was the milk in the bottle. She told me that I could not leave my seat until I described what I saw and to keep looking closely. So I was twitching and fidgeting, and about to cry when it dawned on me that there was a line, a quarter-inch wide, separating the top from the bottom. I noticed that the milk at the top was a little darker than the milk at the bottom. She nodded, pleased, saying, "That's right, son. That's the *cream* on top of the milk." So I asked her what cream is and she explained that the cream is the essence, the sweetest, thickest, most nutritious and best part of the milk. This was before we became accustomed to the distilled, homogenized milk we buy today.

She then shook the bottle forcefully, set it back in front of me and asked me again what I saw. I noticed immediately that the line was gone and all the milk looked the same. I said, "That was a neat trick, Grandma." She smiled and told me to sit there and keep looking. I must have sat there a full ten minutes gazing at that bottle. I was squirming, antsy and on the verge of tears again because I really wanted to get up and do anything else but sit there staring at that milk.

Then it hit me. The line was back. At some point while I wasn't looking the cream had risen back to the top of that bottle. I shouted, "Grandma, it's back. The cream is back on top. How did you do that?" She smiled and said, "The cream is the essence and the best part of the milk, and it always rises to the top. You, my son, are the cream of humanity. All humanity started with your ancestors in Africa and don't you ever forget it. You are neither a nigger nor a Negro. You are an African, the father of civilization and descendant of kings and queens. You are the cream of this planet and just like that cream rose to the top of that milk bottle, you will rise back to the top of civilization, because the cream will always rise."

That lesson prompted me to write, years later, in loving memory of my dearest, wonderful grandmother, Thelma "Miss Polly" Johnson:

The Cream Shall Rise

Listen Africans in America

and you shall be told

Of your glorious history

in the days of old

When you were Kings and Queens

of commerce and trade

When the tubs you bathed in

were gold inlaid

When your bodies were covered

with the finest silk

And you drank from silver goblets,

the sweetest milk

When your bedposts were made of oak

and the finest cedar

And the world sought advice

from the African Leader

Yes, listen dear children

and you shall hear

How you sailed the seven seas

without any fear

How you gave the world medicine

and cured those ill

constructed awesome Pyramids

with your mighty will

How when some of the world's people

were still living in caves

Your cities had streetlights

and the roads were paved

Why, when some were scared of fire

and thought the world was flat

You had smoke coming from chimneys

and globes on your floor mats

How we wore the finest rubies

diamonds and pearls

And filled the universities

with our boys and girls

How we introduced writing

so mankind could read

And concerning arts and science

Africans took the lead

Yes listen my people

and you shall know

How you gave the world

splendor a few decades ago

How you built the Sphinx

How you swam the Nile

Then sailed up and down it

To relax for a while

How you marched through storms

Defending God's name

Then wrote laws of anatomy

To contemplate your frame

How you were the first

People to develop speech

Then you created the Griot

So you could learn and teach

Yeah, listen good people

check your history, recall

You carried the torch

that lit the way for us all

And try to remember

as you go through life's maze

That one of these good old

glorious days

You'll be back on top

for the cream shall rise

Just as sure as the sun

lights the eastern skies

THE CREAM SHALL RISE!

Oh, the wisdom of our forefathers and mothers. What has been one of the greatest, most unforgettable gifts bestowed from a beloved elder?

Finding My Voice

BY EUGENE LOVICK

*F*ind *your voice.* The phrase has haunted me ever since I discovered an interest in art. I was told that I would only create mediocre art until I found my voice. The problem was that the human voice was the only voice I knew. So that is where I began.

Words were puzzles to me, so I leaned toward silence. I would come home from school, say hello, go straight to my room and not say another word. And, it was this voice, this mysteriously "absent" voice that spoke what it felt. Although puzzling, it was this voice that helped me choose my medium: visual art. What did painting, photography and sculpture have to do with this voice? The pieces began to come together when I stopped taking the definition of "voice" so literally. This nonvocal voice cleared the way for me to say what I wanted to say visually.

As I searched for my voice, my perception of the world shifted. Slowly my work began to reflect this shift, in style and content. Certain themes became obvious as they obsessively reappeared in my thoughts and in my work—a sure sign that I was on to something. Sometimes the voice spirals a thought into something fuller or serves as a stepping-stone to another idea or area of exploration. I've found my voice through one interest, one curiosity, one exploration at a time.

Listen for your voice, as it is always expressing itself. It's your voice at work when something is on your mind and you can't let it go without talking to a friend about it first. It's your voice calling out when you find yourself interested in a subject that you barely know anything about but now have an insatiable appetite to study. It's your voice speaking when you find yourself in the middle of a place that feels so right, and if you'd been told you'd feel this way, you would have denied it with all of your heart. It's your voice encouraging you when you get a hunch to go somewhere, or doing something on a lark and it leads you to the adventure of a lifetime. It's your voice responding to these words right now as you figure out how they play into what you want to say with all of your being.

We're all born with that voice of joyous, creative expression. It whispers, it screams, and often waits an eternity to be heard. Find your voice and you find everything you are. Find your voice and find yourself.

Consider your voice found. What does it sound like?

A Fire in My Soul

BY KAMAU B. LOVE

It is my ability to love myself unconditionally

in difficult situations that most

challenges me to my core

it is the exercise of love in these fragile times

I know that the outward picture is a reflection of the inner

therefore the impurities of my lower self rise

as the flame of my Soul burns luminous white and violet

My Higher Self is the white light of that flame

shining a light on the impurities and shadows of my lower self

the ego makes every effort to justify its importance

as to why greed, fear and blame can serve me

I know that these elaborate schemes are doomed from the
    start

there is no separation God and I are one

ego stop pretending that I am not connected to the Source

or how I deserve to be rewarded and or punished

This is a perfect moment to be in love I am Love

Everything outward is a perfect

reflection of my inner picture

So, I say let the fire burn until there is only

the purest of Spirit and the sparkle of my Golden Heart

as I choose to love once again.

Always Love B. Love

Journey to Manhood

No matter what the adversity
Or who the adversary,
You are the bigger man.

—Curtis V

The Ideology of the Lean

BY RANDALL HORTON

I'm thinking to myself *Superfly* the first time I see

Pocketknife bend the corner between history and

algebra class, almost hugging the brick wall with his

right shoulder, the stringent sway of his left arm like

a well-oiled piece of machinery in search of a brace

to propel his half-bounce strut. Although his strides

are not long, each time he thrusts the bow of his legs,

then drag pigeon-toed feet forward, the circular crack

of space revealed speaks of contempt, a trait that will

always keep him unchained. So I emulate his defiance,

practicing in front of full-length mirrors anywhere I can;

perfect my own variation of the lean until it feels natural

and I can express my entire belief system in a walk.

Degrees of Separation

BY WILLIE HOBBS

In the mornin', before I catch up with my boys, I watch
from the bus circle, watch you get outta yo' raggedy red
Honda Civic with yo' briefcase, scratchin' yo' navel
through yo' shirt and double-checkin' to see if you locked
yo' car.

I check it too, after you run to class. I would tell you that,

but you'd think I was tryin' to steal it, but that's alright—

coach.

Dressed like church and smellin' like the mall—that's what
    I told my momma 'bout you

and how you hate me callin' you

coach.

I skip most of my classes except for yours and PE. Shop class
    be straight, too…sometimes.

I say dumb stuff in class to see what you'll do. Most people
    that dress like you

be scared of me, but you diff'rent,

coach.

I know everybody in class think I'm retarded 'cause they
    say "Dr. Hobbs" and I don't.

But they don't jump slick in my face 'cause I'll kick
    somebody to sleep. Oh my bad,

I would *beat a person up very badly*… Man, it's been, like, just
    me and *my ma*

for the longest and I been playin' football forever, so,

any black man ever wondered how I was doin' always
   been a coach

I know, I know, you worked all them years for them master
   degrees...

You *a doctor,* not a coach.

But I'm just sayin' though, why cain't you be both,

for me?

The Dumb Class

BY REGINALD LOCKETT

They didn't use

nice terms like

learning disabled to describe

us, the students in Miss Cornish's

basement classroom

at Longfellow Elementary

next to the storage rooms

where the janitors

kept big push brooms, mops,

buckets, and huge barrels

of industrial cleansers, soap,

and wax.

We were just dumb, retarded

or slow, embarrassments

to brothers, sisters, and cousins

who disowned us the second

their feet entered

the schoolyard gate.

I was the youngest at seven

and the only one in the right grade.

The others were older, like Carlene,

fresh from Arkansas, who was twelve

in the third grade, dipped snuff,

and chewed tobacco;

Theodis, who was fourteen

in the fifth and kept

being held back because

he spent most of the year

locked up at juvenile hall;

and Billy Boo, who was sixteen

in the sixth and wore a wavy process

teased into a big pompadour,

and had a ditty-bop walk.

That year,

while Miss Cornish read

Better Homes and Gardens

and let the class run wild,

I taught myself to write

in longhand and how to do

third, fourth, and fifth grade arithmetic

after the new colored school nurse

discovered I needed glasses,

a pair of glasses.

Jujitsu, Pain and the Life of Black Men

BY WILLIE HOBBS

Ashanti and I bowed and entered the modest Yawara *dojo* (the place of training for martial arts) in sweats, mouths dry with nervous excitement. Ashanti, my son, was five at the time. He squeezed my hand with excitement at the sight of the children his age doing exercises on the mat, all dressed in identical *gis* (martial arts uniforms) and rather focused. Nunchuckas, swords and tournament trophies were high on the wall like family pictures.

"Ooo! Dassa kung-fu, Daddy?"

"Mmm-hmm."

Ashanti is big-hearted, trusting and cursed with my heavy

eyelashes and smooth skin. Now that he was a kindergart-
ner in a very public school, the same tests that haunted me
were now taking hold of him. His toys were suddenly dis-
appearing into a chickenpox-scarred, overweight and snag-
gletoothed vortex of a schoolyard bully.

"What you mean that boy took your Power Ranger?"

"Uhhh, I mean, I was going to give it to him. I mean, I
mean I let him hold it."

"Get it back. Tomorrow."

"But, ummm. Well, never mind."

Ashanti's bully problem was a metaphor for everything
that stared me down in life. I began staying up at night
reliving missed childhood opportunities at payback, all
brought on by my son's tribulations. I wanted both my son
and I to learn how to make folks eat their breakfast through
IVs...*for real.*

I'm only one and a half generations from the kinfolk who
have fish fries, get drunk and fight each other. Having been
removed from the eye of such storm, word sparring was the
closest I got to real brawling. I never got around to throwing
jaw hinge-cracking blows. Words were my reaction after
flinching, parrying off or diffusing confrontations. Humor
was my fighter's Vaseline, keeping reality from cutting too
deep into the skin. And I've kept it caked on thick, the kind
of thick that turns a beard sticky-gray.

I brought my son and myself to the Yawara Dojo to face this issue head-on. I spent my teenage years wading through the androgynous eighties and the "run-and-tell-who's-in-charge" reasoning of a well-meaning, middle-class, female-run household. However, in the corner of every hallway, movie theater and house party there seemed to lurk hardened, stitched-up black boys—the loud-talking Tyrones, Reginalds, Ray-Rays and Reds who regarded being held back a grade as a chance to rule a year longer. They were the ones who turned from the urinal and pissed on people's sneakers for the hell of it. And nearly every one of them seemed to pick me and my maternally inspired conflict-resolving skills from the herd when they felt the need to maintain their reputations.

I quickly realized I was missing a sharp, unbending directness in my dealings with people. I found most of my refuge from the ruthlessness of the teenage social sphere in writing poetry and drawing portraits of cars, pit bulls and well-endowed women. People constantly assumed I was a girl because of my Afro, soft skin and long eyelashes. No other boy seemed to have my long, fluttering fingers either, fingers remaining unusually soft from constant dishwashing chores. The years of second-stringing it in peewee tackle football could do only so much to toughen a brother. Lifting weights and *third*-stringing it in junior varsity as a one-hundred-and-seventy-pound noseguard didn't cut it either.

There was an awe-inspiring, senseless cruelty eluding me, a meanness I was unable to muster to save my life. Girls, especially the black ones, quickly followed suit with the "thugs" in order to get at the top of the social food chain. To keep from being "dissed," I remained quiet, aside from an occasional witty retort that would roll from my tongue from out of nowhere.

Still, the accusations of being a Punk trailed me at every standoff with restless black folks, usually males whose ultimate resolve seemed to stand on the question of whether I could kick their behinds. This seemed to be the case even with relatives, making family reunions with pistol-toting grandfathers and Miller High Life–swigging uncles frightening encounters. Sure, I got my hands on a few people. There were just *way* more people I could've gotten, should've gotten. Way more! But I was too afraid to incur pain, or worse, to inflame an already tense situation trying to defend myself.

I set out to correct my passiveness through the Yawara *Dojo*. Our teacher or *sensei,* was a diminutive, bald man from the Virgin Islands. *Sensei* bowed as my son and I sat by the mat. We were going to learn the system of jujitsu, how to focus and make the most of the next "unavoidable opportunity." The teacher had seen me struggling at the local community center under the instruction of a brother who'd rather sell burned CDs and calling cards than teach his students. Granted, the classes were free, but how many times can an instructor ask his students to punch in a horse stance while he checks his cell phone to see who's coming out to the club with him later that night? A Virgin Islander and several of his professional-looking, dreadlocked students came in to visit the class and after a month or so, left. I thought I was doomed to doing unending combinations until he called my house.

"We are located at Tharpe Street now, across from Raa Middle—in the little building next to Domino's."

I didn't even know if I could afford it. "Bet, I'll be there."

It didn't take long for me to see that, at one-eighty, I was the thickest cat in the place.

This was encouraging until I got passed around to smaller students in the dojo practicing throws. It took a while to learn to strike the mat when landing, so the impact wouldn't sting (as much). I did get my fun on, too. I got a bit overzealous once or twice. Jaro, one of the dreadlocked guys, pulled my collar.

"It isn't a strongman contest," he said. "It's about proper balance and focusing the natural energy."

Ah, I thought, some of that *Way of the Dragon* poetry mess (Did I mention that I was heavier than this dude, probably by forty pounds or so?). *He's little. Of course he thinks it ain't about brute strength!*

"Here, let me show you."

Jaro threw me on the mat as if I were a bothersome backpack full of Shakespeare anthologies. I got up, massaged my hip and looked around to see if Ashanti saw it.

"I'm not sure if I applied the technique properly." Jaro motioned me to come closer. "Once again."

I stepped back from him. "Naw. Naw. You got it right."

Four months of being thrown, learning to fall and joint locking followed. I discovered my running from pain actually made blows more excruciating. Aikido joint locks were practiced that, if you tensed up, would hurt enough to make you stay home the following week. I sat home for a week with an ice pack on my wrist, staring out of the window on a rainy day when I realized expecting the worst of a situation seemed to affect other facets of my life: fearing something will happen and attracting that very thing had haunted me since middle school.

I sparred and noticed a tendency to talk myself up for adversity—nearly hyperventilating—with the manic energy you find in a boxer warming up for a fight. After wearing myself out bouncing around and taking a heel in the gut from being too tired to block it, I learned—the harder the head, the tougher the lesson. With practice, I learned to calm down, breathe and patiently focus while looking for an opening, then taking it.

Jujitsu's "mind no mind" concept was an eye-opener. Rather than trying to analyze everything before I made a move, I had to learn to move freely, trusting that I was connected with my own instincts. When second-guessing oneself, everything freezes, forcing one out of the poetics of motion, out of the "zone." I watched my son fearlessly hurl himself across the mat. Still fresh in the world, I envied the way he naturally took to the *sensei*'s instruction. I watched him and wanted to be a kid again, full of "Why can't I?" Now my greatest visualization is to express my physical power with the efficiency I strive for in my words.

It's the same thing in life. I've held back approaching women, fearing imperfection or embarrassment, only to find things would have actually gone in my favor had I stepped up. There's a stack of unread writing-conference brochures on my desk at home. I'm fearful of being hit in the face with rejection should I commit to applying.

"Kaaai!"

My first front punch in my *gi* felt awkward but official. My son sat on the bench, smiling with pride. His bare feet kick-paddled out from his new *gi* pants.

"Kaaai!"

"Do it some again, Daddy!"

"Kaaaai!"

Ashanti elbowed the little girl next to him. "I can do dat."

I started getting into it to prove to my son that if I could do it, he could, too. I realized his confidence overshadowed my dreams of trying the punches, kicks and joint locks out on past enemies.

"Oww, man! That's my arm!"

One day I was in the kitchen messing with my wife. She came at me, playfully, with a sudsy spatula. Toying around, I did a hakko ryu jujitsu maneuver and the spatula wound up on the floor by the fridge. The suds were splattered across her feet; she was in an arm bar. I noticed my shoulders had no chance to tense up. There was no time to cloud my head with unnecessary thought. There was no chance to question simplicity. I was just being.

I wondered why I had never experienced this "just being" state when I ventured into a judo or shaolin class in my preteen years. I now realize my father, when he was around, was intimidated by the kicks and punches. He'd find the smallest reason to step into my space, so close his toes would be on top of mine, daring me to move. The index finger thumped at my chest bone, to make sure I fell back with my feet still trapped under his.

"I got yo' karate for you!" he would bark.

I was forced to stop judo and shaolin before even reaching the yellow-belt level. The excuse always came from him and was sometimes as trivial as forgetting to do the dishes. I internalized his uneasiness as something inherently wrong with me. After all, simple slap boxing with friends on my way to the mall would have a police black and white pulling over to the curb, quizzing us on who we were and where we were headed. Such aggression made the women of the family nervous when my brother and I wrestled in the living room. Some furniture was sure to break, proving that kind of foolishness was too much of a liability.

I am hell-bent on building Ashanti's spirit and mind to prepare him for life in a way I never enjoyed. I see jujitsu keeping my boy from being scarred. He will learn its rough-housing aspects enough to earn the respect of knuckleheads, and get beyond being paralyzed by pain. He will be respect-ful and have class, yet be manly enough to keep from bruising like a peach over life's challenges. He will know the balance, so will I. By training together, our relationship grows stronger.

No one clowns white belts in this *dojo*. Everyone is treated with respect. I can mess up a move and the world will continue turning. Through our *sensei,* I can see that violence—at least the threat of it—has its place and is glo-rified only by the ignorant. Despite the feminist hooey I get at home from my wife, testosterone is far from an evil chemical I need to downplay. It has its place.

Two more months have passed. I have turned thirty-one years old, and Ashanti is six. We are about to take our yellow-belt tests, and I'm not concerned. Along the way, I've learned discipline, self-assurance and humility. I've learned how to catch myself when I'm getting short with Ashanti's faults. We're both growing, keeping it all in balance.

Jujitsu answers a lot of questions. As I learned to pull my punches and kicks for female jujitsu students I spar with, I've also learned to release them more freely with the men. But, more importantly, I understand that many of the enemies in my past knew nothing of degrees of force. Some were ignorant. Some knew of no other way to see if I possessed any heart. Young boys are insecure but have a sense of warrior in them. Their journey is unfocused, devalued and hap-hazardly shucked off by society. The bully we call life looks to see if we'll flinch or stand firm. How many friendships between black men were initiated with them talking loud with their hands in each other's faces, as stupid as that sounds. We all struggle to find our way. Only now, my son and I can stand—in mind and spirit—and see trouble to its end.

Granted, this new understanding of humanity doesn't keep me from dropping my eyes to somebody's chin or solar plexus when they are ticking me off. Enlightenment doesn't mean you are numb to things. You simply have a better idea of what is going on within and without. Just *knowing* these nasty jujitsu combinations, I can peel my top lip from my teeth to form a sick kind of smile—the same kind of smile my son had on his face the day he came home with his long-lost Power Ranger.

How might I spent quality time with a child—my own or others in my village—that could build discipline, community, strength, character or self-confidence, while strengthening our relationship?

Remains of the Day

BY JAMES E. CHERRY

During the remains of the day,

Speeding through a major artery that

Leads from the inner city to suburbia, a scene

down side streets, dark with isolation and

obscurity, arrests my eye from a backward

glance, indelible images of

hooded night riders with hangman's noose.

Three police cars have subdued a late-model

Mercedes and three cops, white, have

Cornered a suspect, black, face downward,

Handcuffed with a knee growing out of his back.

Thoughts, like a flashbulb of paparazzi, blind

my mind's eye to robbery suspect, mass

murderer or the simple misdeed of being Black

in America, as I sit behind the wheel of my sports

car, prescribed medication for chronic back pain

on the seat beside me, easing off the accelerator,

while nightfall descends like a funnel cloud,

realizing that I've been traveling this

same road in this same life for way too long.

Do you know someone who's been done an injustice, who's now physically, mentally or emotionally imprisoned? Call out his or her name and write a prayer of love, compassion and salvation....

Written Before Birth

BY MICHAEL BURT

A typical Black man's life

is already written before birth

Sent to the publisher,

released, and on the shelves

before contractions are felt

The back of this novel

does not summarize me

It does not revisit my

thesis: I am a successful Black man

No good, no ambition, simply procrastination

Summoned to the Ghetto

with no way of emancipation

Shaking hands with him,

them, and her

until all I have is gone

Not realizing I sold

my soul to the man

at the bottom

Won't graduate from high school

got a baby on the way

No one will hire me

Momma suggests a GED

but that is embarrassing

I'd rather live in her basement

no change needed

no replacement either

At this rate I'll marry

the cemetery

in an early grave

Then probably be charged

and convicted of rape

since I smiled at his daughter

which pissed off her father

Will steal your luxuries

kill your families

shame your ancestors

and disgrace your race

because this life was chosen for me

it was written before birth

I have decided, made up my mind

It has shown through my life

I will Stand

I will not fit the criteria

assume the position

succumb to the pressure

confirm the stereotypes

or be the type

that becomes what they

want me to become

Don't forget where you came from...

I am a successful Black man

When They Came To Take Him

BY REGINALD LOCKETT

In memory of Robert Garner

When they came for him,

it wasn't the gentility

of his tastefully painted, neat

single-level Victorian house

tucked away

in a decent neighborhood

they saw.

When they came to take him,

it wasn't the meticulously

restored vintage Jaguar

in the garage or the shiny MG

parked in the driveway

they noticed.

When they came

to subdue him, it wasn't

the eclectic choice of furniture,

original paintings, sculpture,

and prints

they studied in awe.

When they entered his space,

uninvited, to force on him

their lopsided wills,

it wasn't the impressive library

that covered an entire wall

or the careful selection

of jazz classics

that trained their cold,

insensitive gazes.

When they came

to confront him,

it wasn't the chic tie,

conservative tweed,

and handmade shoes

he wore they came

dressed in blue

to out flaunt.

When they came

to exercise the powers

vested in them to uproot him

from his own being,

it wasn't the Master of Arts,

secure job with a bank,

and superb fiction

and criticism he wrote

they took into consideration

that morning

on the last day in May.

When they came

to capture his spirit

and erase his vision,

it wasn't the intelligence

in his eyes,

the pride in his face,

and the gentleness

in his voice

they wanted to see.

No.

All they saw was

he was black,

believed armed and dangerous,

and resisting arrest

when they fired

a 12-gauge riot pump,

point-blank,

dead off in his chest.

Here I Stand a Better Man

BY COREY WHITE

If you had X-ray vision you would feel weak in the knees
just by looking at my heart

Then could you imagine watching my brain and there
stands millions of crows just picking it apart

My hands are nearly raw from the numerous hands that I
have shaken

My skin is darker from the hands that have walked away
and burned my skin with their jealous looks

Can you imagine my eyes that have seen things that
GOD himself would be ashamed to see

Could you ever envision looking into the mirror and by
what has been done saying to yourself "Man this isn't me"

My ears are burning constantly from hearing all the
dreams and hopes but are only lies

From having other people's world placed on my
shoulders I have better strength within my thighs

My stomach is full of a special flying dust from being
filled with constant butterflies

Can you imagine fingernails bitten down to the nubs as
I would watch my dreams and plans crumble right
before my eyes

My back is sensitive to mattresses now for having laid on
a mattress for a crime I didn't commit for nearly a year

Could you imagine my feet filled with blisters because of
the many miles I have walked trying to reach my goals
yet they still don't seem near

If you could see how swollen my knees are from the
many, many, many times that I have knelt and prayed

My pockets are filled with hollow air due to the many
times I have done people wrong the debts that
I have paid

My hair has faded in some spots from the many times the
disarray had me not knowing where I was at

Could you imagine the confidence nearly taken away
from the many times I've heard people laugh

My ankles have chipped bones from the many obstacles
I've had to jump over

My arms are longer than average because when I recognized
someone as an enemy I would reach out and say, "Please
not another step closer"

My eardrums are swollen from the constant beating of
the echoes of lies against me

My lungs are worn, torn from the constant letting the old
out trying to gain a new inner by letting the old go
and be

I'm dehydrated from the constant tears that at points
seemed would never stop flowing

The part of my skin that is not burned shows the stretch
marks of how I am forever growing

My memory is forever filled with the vision of a thief as he
or she stands before me constantly saying,
"A thief I'm isn't"

My piggy bank is full of rusted pennies that I have taken
back out of the wishing wells when I didn't get my
wishes

Could you imagine my kidneys run down by thinking
what I was drinking would finally cleanse my soul

To have been put in the situations I have been put in you
would see why my blood reaches a boiling point then
drops off to a chilling cold

If you could feel the pain I feel in my neck from having
to constantly look over my shoulder

Could you imagine having elbows that ache so from flexing my arms to the sky and yelling, "Take me now I don't want to become another day older"

I would be hard pressed to get you to believe after all the aches and pains I have no ill will because I realize now it was all a part of me to have a greater plan

I now pass this on to you because

Here I Stand A Better Man

Today, how do I stand as a better man?

Things You Should Know: A Letter to My Son

BY OPAL PALMER ADISA

Darling JaJa:

Only seventeen, but you are a man, and a man of whom I am proud, as you juggle your part-time job as peer-sex educator with your zeal for soccer, and maintain a 3.0 grade-point average in school. I know you are a little anxious as you enter this final year in high school and try to identify which colleges might be right for you. Know I am here, within reach, to assist you in this process. Recognize that you have my perpetual support and love.

I see so much of me in you, and perhaps that is why

we clash sometimes. Like me, you are ruthlessly independent, don't want to be told anything, very emotional, and private too. But I also see a lot of your father in you, and perhaps that is also why we clash sometimes. Like him, you are a perfectionist, single-minded in task, resent intrusion, and always want to put forth your best.

I also see you, so different from your father or me, so dissimilar from your two bossy sisters between whom you are sandwiched. You are sensitive, loving, often willing to concede your position to avoid conflict and bring about resolution. I also observe your resilient personality, but what is most admirable is your wisdom—your ability to tell great stories, like an elder, that leave us all amazed at your knowledge and deep, spiritual understanding of life.

Most endearing of all is your willingness and ability to mend bridges when we disagree. Although you might storm into your room, after a while, when you have had some peaceful, reflective time, you come to me, and say, "Mommy, can we talk about this now?" or "Mommy, I am sorry I acted the way I did."

I love how when you are not feeling well, or sometimes, even when you don't want to talk and I am in my bedroom reading, you come and lie on my bed, and we are just quiet together, communicating without talking. I love that you feel comfortable to talk to me about sex, the first time you smoked and feeling overwhelmed with school, extracurricular activities and all the other things that life tosses at you at this age, living in an urban environment. I am honored that we have that love and connection still, and I want you to know how much I value and hold sacred this shared space between us.

I will always be available to you, free of judgment with unconditional love. I am prepared to listen without interrupting or offering solutions, ready to comfort and suggest practical advice when solicited, or help you with time management, and be your coach and friend. I want you to know I am always approachable and you can come to me whenever and under any and all circumstances. I pledge that I will always listen and be a sounding board for you.

Because I am a single mother, I have sometimes stumbled into believing the erroneous hype that as a woman I cannot teach you how to be a man, but I now know that is not true, a gross misconception. I am as competent and as worthy a teacher as your father or any other positive man because I know intimately the qualities of manhood. More importantly, I model righteous-

ness, confidence, self-assuredness, and ultimately that is
what manhood is about. I wrote the following poem in
your honor, and in support of my role as your mother
who will do whatever it takes to see you firmly on your
own as a positive, responsible, contributing member of
society.

What Can A Mother Teach Her Son?

i can teach him the length

and depth of love

and if that's the only lesson

he learns

he's ahead of the game

even though i'm not a man

i can teach him

that a man who loves and respects himself

reciprocates without fear

i can teach him honesty

i can teach him pride

i can teach him to trust his instincts

to value his life and his goals

i can teach my son to be a man

because being is man

is to be a caring

self-determined human being

And JaJa, if I do nothing else, if I give you nothing more than the above lesson, then my role in your life, as your mother and your teacher to walk your path with grace and peace, has been effective and well worth all my efforts.

In our family, you serve as a beacon for your younger male cousins, allowing them to see through you, that with focused energy and dedication, they too can achieve their life goals; that being a young man is to be mannerly, polite and even soft-spoken, a direct contrast to much of the hip-hop-thug-gangster mentality that most of the music videos portray; that to be down doesn't mean to be pimpin', or to be hanging out on the corner hollering at girls, or wearing pants to your knees, dropping out of school; that in fact the very down brothers are you and your peers, who are nicely dressed, take pride in education, respect your parents and yourselves and are intent on making significant contributions to society. The really down brothers are you and your boys who know your history and are comfortable and able to move in all worlds and hold your own, not by selling out, or through other self-depreciating actions. You know who you are. You know your lineage. You understand that others have sacrificed for you.

As a brother of two sisters, you make me so proud when I hear you say that when you are out with your sisters, you stand at their backs, protecting them from young men who are disrespectful, who attempt to make inappropriate advances and who ogle at their behinds. You know so well about defending family, and what it means to be a man and to protect the home front.

When you are out with me, I am so honored to introduce you as my son to my friends and acquaintances who congratulate me on how mannerly you are, and I am delighted at how at ease and comfortable you are among my peers.

And although sometimes you get frustrated and put yourself down unnecessarily, or compare yourself to your big sister or to others, I want you always to value and affirm your special, unique traits that make you the remarkable young man that you are, especially at this season in our history when black people, especially young black men, are under attack, made the scapegoat with too few true role models to emulate. You are truly a shining example, praised and accepted by your girlfriend's parents, loved and supported by all your grandparents, aunts and cousins.

Don't ever forget, not even for a moment, who you are and that your life, all that you enjoy and take for granted, is the result of the unimaginable efforts of all your ancestors, maternal and paternal, and their determination to continue the legacy.

Don't forget or neglect to hone all your talents, not just soccer, but also your visual, artistic abilities, your dancing, and your ability to make people laugh.

Don't ever allow others or your own fears to immobilize you or limit your vision, because the world is truly yours. As you have had the opportunity to travel to many different countries in the world, know there are many places, outside of the U.S., where you can live in dignity and unity with others.

Don't ever allow disappointments to cause you to withdraw or to become small, or to become a victim— seeking drugs as solace and plunging into despair.

Don't become narrow-minded or put other people, their traditions, religious beliefs or language down.

Live life with gusto and zeal, JaJa.

Love as fiercely as I love you, even more.

Welcome others into your life. Life is truly as fantastic as you make it.

Always remember that all mistakes and setbacks are learning opportunities that will ultimately lead to your growth and personal advancement if you don't falter or get stuck.

Dream big and never, never accept defeat. Dream and never allow anyone to tell you that you want too much or that you are reaching too high. Reach higher still. Dream bigger dreams.

Have a spiritual base that is inclusive, connects you with others, and grounds you in the one truth of the immense, limitless miracles in life.

Be mindful of the physical earth and your role to protect and keep it safe and healthy for the next ten generations that will come after you.

Let joy be your guide. Share it and give it away freely, and wrap yourself in it.

Avoid negative, pessimistic people who are apt to say, "No, it's not possible." Make a liar out of them. Illuminate their doubts.

Trust your instincts and nurture your ability to discern. The maxim All that glitters isn't gold is very relevant in these times when there are so many facades, shams, talk and the outward appearance of grandeur. Be real and go for what is real, regardless of fashion or appearances.

Mostly, be happy. Be happy, be ecstatically happy and enjoy your life, and sometimes that might mean being willing to be a buoy bouncing in the ocean.

Walk Good & One Love,

Mommy

If your mother could write a letter to you today, what would she have said she's most proud of?

Lunch with Brother

BY JAMES E. CHERRY

Mike had arranged lunch on a Monday afternoon at a
   popular deli trendy with the college set

and the buzz of business deals of men with well-

trimmed beards in blue suits and red neckties.

He is my older brother and has been thinking

about words and their correlation to his life,

desiring to document his rise into entrepreneurship,

now wearing success like a three-piece Italian suit.

Not very long ago home was the helplessness of public

housing, but today it's gated communities on the other

side of town, real estate reserved for

athletes, doctors, bankers.

I order a Reuben on rye; he settles for a salad, words

not being the only thing on his mind. Idle chatter

solidifies into outlines, titles, structure, chapters,

publishers and I see the answered prayers of my mother

from the light in his eyes and my father's determination

in profile the way Mike cocks his head at an angle

when I warn of copyrights, agents and editors.

Conversation dissipates into politics, sports, mutual

funds, a half-eaten Reuben (eyesight more voracious

than appetite) and chocolate ice cream for dessert.

Outside, we exchange comments on the weather and

promises to sit down with tape recorders for the sake

of posterity before we embrace and shake hands, a

generation of dreams converging in the space

where our flesh presses together.

Journey to Fatherhood

The birth of a child,
is the growth of a boy,
that has just become a man…

—Michael J. Burt

Giggles Missed

BY MARIA D. DOWD

She stood at the door swatting that one pain-in-the-butt fly. It was the perfect outdoor day. Behind her, hopeful hearts pounded with anticipation of just a glimpse of his sandals because they sensed what was about to go down, again. Her wide hips were hugged by a sleeveless used-to-be church dress, now too tight around her growing waist, and dishpan hands that carried far more years than her face because she'd not ever been told to preserve their tender caress with latex. She only knew what she needed and the rest of it wasn't paying nobody's bills or putting milk in the fridge. He walked up knowing what he already knew, because the folded, then unfolded, unmailed check attached to that whisper of an account and the hope that tomorrow's search would be more fruitful still sat on the nightstand in the apartment he now shared with the late-night boom of way too much bass and aloneness. The rent was two weeks late, thanks to the unemployment office. And, she wasn't smiling, never did she smile…not now, not anymore. Neither did the landlord, whose frowns she was growing weary of, not to mention the notices held by tape on the front door for everybody to see.

All he wanted to do was spend the day in the park with his son and daughter, both named after him, more or less, born into a time when happiness (and a steady paycheck) overrode the challenges of life in a city where more and more jobs—including his last one—were shipped overseas. He had bus fare and burger money for all three, the green grass and playgrounds were for the taking, and he'd heard on the news that there was going to be a show in the amphitheater with clowns, puppets and magicians.

He missed them dearly. He missed their little fists that all but tickled his back as he tackled them to the floor like fuzzy kittens. They'd kick up those tennis shoes that lit up their shadows when they tried not to step on cracks, and they cracked up until tears kissed their cheeks, their voices grew hoarse and the youngest cried, "I gotta pee!" And, he'd sweep the little one up in his arms and whisk him off to the potty, where he'd so proudly show his dad how he could use it like a big boy, standing…oh, but aided and aimed…so that Momma wouldn't have a fit when she got home from the restaurant across town later that night, looking for undone chores and a potty that needed rinsing. He discovered he enjoyed being Mr. Mom, although he had a lot to learn about multitasking, a title he stumbled into after the irregularity of his income became a festering source of discontent…then separation, even after the test came back positive.

She was fed up with the struggle and started praying for something or someone different. If she had to struggle, she might as well do it by herself. Because of his failings, he'd resolved that she did deserve something or someone different, but why wedge herself between the babies and him? Was currency more important than their contentment? Was money more important than their time together? Yeah, he could certainly be more mindful of his time and beers at the bar around the way, but he had to drown out the nights with R&B because he couldn't bear the thinning air and not hearing the lyrical soothing of their self-assured voices demanding his attention.

"Daddy, play this with me."

"Daddy, can you watch *The Lion King* with us?"

Now, their singsongs sounded off tune and pained, and it made him want to cry.

"Daddy, when are you going to come get us?"

"Daddy, I miss you. Can you take me to your house?"

"Daddy, Momma says you can't come today. Why?"

As he approached the front porch and saw the pinches in the corners of her mouth, his neck grew warm. Fingering the loose change and dollar bills in his pocket, he waited for the expected. Then her "hi" and rescind of the park visit spewed from her frustrated-tasting mouth, sticking to his heart like hot tar. Then he heard their cries. Then she felt the stir of his (or her) kick. Her tired hands touched the expansive belly and his weathered ones were thrown up, pushing every single moment like this one into the lining of some forgotten realm. Then the remains of his near-empty pockets landed at her feet. She yelled a few more things that he's certain landed like explosions on all three sets of innocent ears. Vowing in his mind to return with the rent once his check came in, it was canceled by the moan in his achy head that questioned how he could continue to face the faces of his two little namesakes, more or less, and the one he'd hope to see emerge on his or her birthday, with too loud of a reminder that he was *always* coming with not enough? This time, her *don't come back* until it's more took on new meaning.

Too little had become too much. And, the jobs were sporadic at best. Not surprisingly, his unshaven, unsaved face got lost in the sea of lost faces of fathers wearing the shame of missed giggles, birthdays, visits to the park and trips down memory lane of brighter days of teaching how to ride bikes and evenings eating popcorn and watching *The Lion King* for the hundredth time.

Seas and seas of missed opportunity to share his childhood stories and life experiences; of his funny jokes and serious talks; of his heavy hand and light heart; of his empathy with his sons; and protection of his daughters; and of his ability to love like only a father can.

Trials of Divorce: An Open Letter

BY 7VN

Forwarded via e-mail yesterday

Dear Ex-wife,

You may not want to hear from me, but instead of worrying about that, spirit has led me to forward this e-mail I just got from my frat to you, telling the story of three men, rushing to the gate at an airport, over-turning a cart of apples belonging to a blind girl. Faced with the choice of catching the flight versus turning around to help the girl, two chose to catch the flight, and the third man returned to help her. He found the girl on her hands and knees, crying and hopelessly groping for her produce as people swirled around her. He turned the cart right side up, picked up the apples that had rolled everywhere, then gave her money to replace the fruit that had been battered and bruised. The girl asked the kind man if he were Jesus. With that question burning in his soul, he turned to catch his flight home. The message is for all of us to live, walk and act as He would. Be kinder than necessary, for everyone you meet is fighting some kind of battle.

I'm not even sure you'll get this e-mail. You changed our house phone number without telling me or giving me the new number, much less providing me with your new e-mail address to keep in regular contact with you regarding our children. Since you've been taking "cutting all ties" so literally, if you get this, then it was meant to be. If not, oh well. One way or another, you need to get this message that the Universe is sending out to you....

Since I've known you, you've talked about not wanting your soul to go to hell, about living a righteous life. You read the Bible when you feel like it, listen to televangelists on Sundays, even go to church now and then, yet you continue to behave the way that you do toward your children and me. Being unreasonable is something God would frown upon, not to mention the fact that it can block blessings that would otherwise come to you in your life over time. Whether in your efforts to build your new business, or move on in your life with other relationships, don't you realize how karma works and that God is watching ALL your actions, not just the ones that YOU want Him to see?

A lot of the things that you're doing are so unnecessary and you probably never stop to think what would happen if the shoe were on the other foot. One day it might be, and how you would want to be treated is what you have to consider. I know you may be hurt. I am, too. But I'm not using hurt feelings as an excuse to be disrespectful or be mean to you. Much of what has gone on since my departure is because you forced my hand, as I got tired of being backed into a wall, slighted and treated like I had no parental rights. At one time, you said you loved and respected me, but as of late, I have seen nothing to indicate that there was ever any TRUE love there.

By badmouthing me in front of our children and keeping them from seeing me when I want to, you were depriving and hurting them more than me, whether you know it or not. In good conscience, I can't just sit back and watch that happen. I told you that no court could ever make me do more for my children than I was willing to do myself. I've been the best father that I can be. And I intend to stand up for our children! So I'll be seeing you in court next month and every month after that until I get custody of my two boys. The sooner you can accept the fact that just because WE couldn't be doesn't mean OUR children should have to suffer from your anger and frustrations, the better off we will all be. Until then, be clear that I'm digging in for the long haul to pursue this custody issue with passion because I'm doing what I genuinely feel is best for our children's lives.

There is some justice, I pray, in this system that was not designed to be my friend, but considering what the stakes are, I'm willing to go for mine. The whole spirit of the boys is totally uplifted when I'm around versus when I'm not. That's something that I want to see grow, and I want to see it up close and personal. And since you've chosen to be an obstacle to that, unfortunately I must go over you, since I couldn't go through you.

So, before it's too late, I would advise you to reflect on the words in the story above because you just never know what the future may hold and where the chips may fall.

Your EX-HUBBY

ode to our fathers

BY EUNICE HEATH-TATE

we come from men

who understood that fatherhood

was more than spilling life

into women's wombs

men who knew that anger

was never a reason to inflict pain

and a heart bruised or broken

was not an excuse for abuse

men who clearly understood that fear

could never be enough

to abandon their offspring

we come from men

who have long mastered

the art of swallowing tears

men who moved in manly pride

to become breadwinners

sometimes without validation

or support from their women

we come from men who, when

time and time again were slapped

in the face by adversities

stood tall and proud

because they understood

they were the family's backbone

we come from men

who when dishonored and disrespected

chose not to become the missing link

in their children's lives

but instead continued to brace themselves

firmly against a society

that deemed them criminals

branded them endangered species,

stereotyped them lazy and irresponsible

we come from

black men

strong men

brave men

who knew what it meant to be a father

men who understood that a woman's strength

was meant to complement not castrate

Behold the Lilies of the Field

BY GEOFFREY PHILP

Yesterday, as I walked down my driveway to pick up the *Sunday Herald,* I noticed that rain lilies had once again bloomed after a long, dry season in Miami. I've always regarded their appearance as almost miraculous, for it seems as if they do not flower merely because they are watered (I do my fair share of lawn work), but only after rainfall. I surmise that it takes the right sequence of events that includes rainfall, humidity and other factors, and behold, the *Zephyranthes atamasco.*

The appearance of the rain lily also has a special significance for me because it is associated with my father, Sydney George Philp, who I didn't know very well. I was his tenth child from four marriages, so the time that I spent with him was rare, but always important to me. During those brief times together, I came to realize that he was a charming, brilliant man and that, combined with his "high brown" status in Jamaica, must have made him irresistible to the ladies. He also had a great sense of humor.

Anyway, although my teenage years were difficult, our family started Philp get-togethers, which were prompted, sadly, when we found out that our father was ill. We flocked to Jamaica to see the old man and to get to know each other as grown-ups.

My favorite memory of that time was sitting on the veranda with my father and eating roasted corn, smelling the mixture of rain and earth before the showers came tumbling down Long Mountain. Watching him fall asleep as the rain fell, I realized in that moment that even though he might soon not be with us, everything was *irie*.

All has not been forgotten, but forgiven. It had to be that way. The more I talked with my brothers and sisters, especially the ones whom I envied because they had spent so much time with him, I realized that I would not have become the man I am today if the events in my life had not played out in that particular sequence.

My recollection of the rain lily, however, goes back to the time I was leaving the home of his fourth wife to return to

Mona Heights, to the house that he and my mother bought. As I walked with him, he pulled up a rain lily, handed it to me and said, "There, you can't say I never gave you anything." And he laughed.

The old devil laughed.

And all I could do was laugh and tell him that I loved him.

He said, "I know."

So, whenever the rain lilies bloom at my front door, I remember my father and those moments we had together— as brief and miraculous as the appearance of rain lilies.

And, I give thanks.

Everything in Its Time

BY MWALIM (MORGAN JAMES PETERS, I)

As I sit writing this, Charles Wright and the 103rd Street Rhythm Band are telling me, *Express Yourself*. My two-year-old son, Zyggi, alternates between dancing, playing with the EQ switches on the battered old boom box in the corner, and bouncing on his hobbyhorse. My home office has become a playroom. My son's toys share space with a desk, editing deck, books and files. In a couple of minutes, we'll go downstairs and make breakfast. He's already had some juice and a bowl of cold cereal as his early-morning snack while I sipped my coffee. It's Saturday, pancake and turkey sausage morning. It took a year and a quarter to establish the routines of our bachelor pad lifestyle.

How did a carefree, happy-go-lucky writer end up a single custodial parent? It was a classic tale: His mom and I met, fell in love, got married, and had a child. The marriage didn't work and we split. Without running down my ex and her family, I'll suffice it to say that I live in Massachusetts, a notoriously pro-mother state and the court gave me custody of my son, who was eighteen months old and still nursing at the time. While weaning a child can be a difficult task for a mother, it's a virtual impossibility for a father. I now feel fully qualified to detoxify somebody with a chemical dependency, as that is listed among the most hellish experiences of my (and I'm sure my son's) life. Luckily, little ones are adaptable.

One thing I knew for sure, when I was ready to be a parent, I was going to be *ready* to be a parent, emotionally, spiritually and economically. In the early part of my teaching artist career, I became the male role model/surrogate father to several young men who were seeking and needing a man's influence. I could see the impact that I had on these young brothers' lives, as their mothers and grandmothers testified that they seemed to be more mature and responsible after being involved in my program. While absentee fathering is indeed a crisis affecting children across racial and class lines, it's particularly devastating in the communities of color. Children suffer, particularly the boys. Along with a mother's love, it takes the loving guidance and concern of a black man to help our children navigate through the obstacle courses of our society. My parents divorced when I was very young and although my father was involved and influential, he physically wasn't around too much when I was growing up. However, I was lucky enough to have ongoing interaction with influential grandfathers, godfathers, uncles and other extended-family members to offset his absence.

One of the coolest parts about being a professor is having scheduling flexibility. Depending on the semester, I have two to three teaching days during the week. On the other days, I conduct my requisite professional/scholarly activities: writing, shooting films and working on plays. Thus, my son is able to be with me most of the time. The secret to successful parenting is embracing the one thing that I tried to avoid, scheduling and organizing my activities. Once upon a time, I could write or edit films whenever the mood hit. Now it's scheduled around the sleeping schedule of the little man. Of course, I've also found that the quality of my work is much higher because I only have these units of time within which to do my thing.

On nice days, we go out to the park, to the Assonet reservation, or back home to Mashpee where we walk through the woods or go fishing. I look forward to the days when we can go camping. Of course, there are the day-to-day errands. He particularly likes the home improvement stores where they have the race-car shopping carts with steering wheels. As I shop, he "drives." I hadn't realized the impact of these trips on my son until he announced to his mother, "My daddy lives in the Home Depot in Hyannis!" Then there is the nightly ritual Zyggi and I have of dancing to a James Brown, Charles Wright, Grant Green or Parliament Funkadelic song before I put him to bed.

When I was married, a combination of factors prevented me from having the quality of time with my son that I do now. My wife wanted to be a stay-at-home mom, which meant that I had to pick up a lot of side gigs along with my regular teaching duties at the university. She also wanted to control when and how I spent time with our son. Then, my typical working artist's workweek consisted of six to seven part-time jobs to make ends meet. As a musician and theater artist, the nightclub and bar scene was a part of my work environment, where deals were made to secure the next gig. Today, my nightlife mostly involves getting my work done, playing with Zyggi and watching videos.

The drawbacks that I'm finding are mostly in the form of attitudes people have about parenting. Did you know that most men's rooms don't have changing tables? People often assume when I'm out with him that I'm "babysitting." They comment that his mother is so lucky that I'm so good with him, which *obviously* allows her time to get what she needs to do, done. When I was signing us up at the YMCA, completing the paperwork for the single-parent family plan, the woman at the table said, "It's such a shame, little people like him need their mothers." I looked up and said, "I'll dig her up." She stuttered and stammered, weakly tried to explain herself, then disappeared while her coworker finished processing my form.

I realize that I must hug and cuddle a bit more than the average father, and my son is around a lot more "uncles" than most kids, as he comes with me to the Masonic lodge, or to drum practice with the men from the Mashpee Wampanoag tribe.

Has single parenting drastically changed my lifestyle?

Definitely!

Would I change any of it for anything in or out of the world?

Not a chance!

I've been given the privilege by the Almighty and the courts to raise a happy, healthy little boy into a happy, healthy, strong man.

Father's Day 2005

BY James E. Cherry

As you lay there, apparition of the man I feared,

family gathered bedside like priests administering the

last rites of silence, Father's Day has brought me

to this Sunday morning fifteen years late.

Over the past months cancer strengthened, encroached

upon lungs and gray matter, devouring memory of

lessons taught in baiting hooks and casting them with

skill and patience, how to keep my eye on the ball, not

always swinging for the fences and that the main thing

was steadying it between the lines no matter which way

road bent or became dirt and loose gravel to where

ever I was going.

The familiarity of my face had become lost

in the hands of hospice workers skilled in syringes

dulled with morphine and obligation.

As with all things, time reduced the virility of thirty

years of factory labor, the dedication for one woman,

the rearing of seven through discipline, encouragement

and bread to the fragility of skin, bone, a breath at a time.

That evening, with eyes rolled heavenward, you smiled

at the rustling of wings overhead and ascended

to grasp at feathers, your life rising in us

carrying forth promises to a generation of flesh

who will one day dare to speak your name.

The Fabric of This Man

BY MYCHAL SLEDGE

The fabric of this society, within which we all live, is still based in family. However, family, as we once knew it, has changed. Various circumstances have led to the ongoing rise in black female heads of household. Where is the "Proud Poppa" of our families and community? The fact is, we're losing large and viable segments of the black community to prison, public health crises, joblessness, poverty and loss of political power. And these vicious cycles are perpetuated through generations.

It is honorable to be a vital, responsible father. Children need fathers, as much as fathers need their children. A nurturing father is a nurturing man first. I pray and practice

every day to be a better father, and this has brought me unforgettable moments with my children. I had first to realize
that being a father is an awesome gift from the almighty
God.

What is my purpose in their lives and their purpose in
my life?

These precious children, who look like me, talk like me
and imitate me are given to me only for a limited time on
this earth. So, what do I do with this gift?

I can remember being a "drive-by dad." I thought money
was the answer to being a good father. I'd drive by and drop
off gifts for birthdays and holidays, giving false hope and
promises. I believed that I had nothing to contribute but financial support.

For so long I was "sleeping at the light switch." I was con-
sciously dead to the realities of manhood and fatherhood.

I am now a father who heads my household and family.
My willingness to improve myself in life has helped tremendously. I am a leader in my community, an activist and
change agent to many. My children drive me to do more
and be more. And I'm very aware that I'm touching and
reaching the unborn through the teaching of my values and
principles to my children.

The legacy of family will always make a difference in the
community and world we live in. I embrace fatherhood to

lead my family to victory over extinction. My forefathers led, rather than waiting to be led, inspiring me to rise to any challenge that threatens this family I call my own.

Commitment is based on integrity and creditability with self. My children trust me because of my commitment to them. This has allowed me to get them to commit to me and my teachings. The earlier this is established the better. Commitment is doing what I say I am going to do. As a father, the worst thing I can do is give false hope and offer unfulfilled promises. It is wiser to say nothing.

Time together can never be regained. Once it's gone, it's gone. Share quality time together, with no interruptions. It isn't the amount of time that makes a difference, it's the essence of the time we share. Being available is a must, and not just when I want to spend time with them. Their needs come without appointments.

And, as my children's first teacher in life, educating them is another success principle to being a great father. We must give children the correct information and not allow them to be misinformed by others. We must teach our children to put God first, followed by self-preservation, family, friends and community.

Communication is a key success principle of fatherhood. The ability to be able to hear and listen to my children's needs enables me to nurture and support both their needs and wants. Often, I have to open my mind to understand what it was like to be those ages again. The ability to speak to them and not at them critically affects how they receive the messages. And I have learned over the years that it is not only what I say that's important but what I do. Children do what they see, not always what they are told. The example I set for my children—both my sons and daughters—of what a black man is supposed to look like and act like is so important. We are all good talkers, but could we do more?

Real Men Do Cry

BY BILL HOLMES

In a time and place

where heroes were needed

some men unlike yourself

chose not to accept the responsibility

of being a father to their offspring

since the concept of parenthood

scared them to death

never taking into consideration

the ramifications of their actions

upon the lives they brought

into this world

but not you, Sir,

because you stood your ground

determined to build a better life

for your boys where these urban streets

had no names and took no prisoners

and although your marriage to my mother

was neither a bed of roses

nor ended happily ever after

you did your best to blend

our lives with yours

at the expense of

everyone's unique personality

so we could forever be

one happy family.

Unfortunately,

children grow up

too fast and too soon

and have their own dreams to fulfill

and their own lives to live

and too much of anything

will eventually grow sour

especially when it came

to love between father and son

as conflict arose

between you and me

during the awkward years

of my adolescence

where bruised egos

gave way to flaring tempers

and words were exchanged

that took their toll on my self-esteem

fueling my burning anger toward you

for all the hurtful things

you ever said and did to me

I had only one wish

I carried into my adulthood

and that was to inflict

emotional, financial,

physical and psychological pain

upon you until you broke down

and cried before my eyes

because you were the one

who told me that a man

wasn't supposed to cry.

However,

divine intervention

rained on my parade

and interceded with

its own agenda

and the only tears shed

emerged from my eyes

as time began to heal my wounds

I found peace and tranquility

from loving myself

for being the man I am today

and for recognizing

it was finally time

to let go and to leave

the past behind

and although it wasn't easy

it was also time for me

to accept you for who you are

and to forgive you

for the mistakes you made

since I had never walked

in your shoes before

and I couldn't fathom

the things you endured

on the roads you traveled

in life's journey

I tried to understand

that sometimes

people say and do

the wrong things

for the right reasons

because they don't know how

to properly express their love

toward their families

and I too will admit

that I was in the wrong

for all the hurtful things

I said and did to you

over the years

and after all

nobody's perfect.

I have only one request

I ask of you, Sir,

and that is if you ever

look into these eyes

and they appear

to be dampening

please don't mistake

these developing tears

as signs of weakness,

fear or insecurity

but accept them

as expressions of

my pride and joy

and tokens of

my appreciation

that a son has

for his father

and I love you, Dad,

because real men

are neither afraid

nor ashamed

to cry.

Journal

BY VALERIE ANN AYRES

i sit as a distant out-of-town cousin would,

in the corner unsure of what to say or do

cause i'm new in the family & don't want to get in the way.

we're in the room together…alone

he in a shell of himself…body & spirit

with eyes bright as tomorrow's sunshine

but weak as yesterday's news,

explore…search the room. "Where is my son?"

he whispers, in between short, shallow breaths.

i sit in the corner, with a book

keeping my hands busy by turning wordless pages,

remembering

where i had heard that breathing pattern before.

CANCER! is nobody's friend, i think.

in the middle of turning meaningless pages, i pray...

i pray for strength...i pray for him and his son

whom i love and know how he feels at this moment.

his son enters...he wants to hold his hand

i wish i had the camera.

his long slender fingers intertwine with his baby son's hand.

i wonder if he feels the warmth and love that flows

from those fingers...fingers that picked cotton,

molded clay, twice gave in marriage,

upholstered furniture, cut hair, defended

his country/nation & policed his community,

rocked his children, grandchildren...

challenged friends at bones/cards/life,

built homes, rebuilt torn-down fences,

ushered and held the mic in his place of worship,

seized the Bible with such tenderness, brought tears to your
eyes…

i don't need to wonder…they hold hands for hours.

i sit in the corner witnessing love pour from father into son

through their intertwined fingertips as they watch history
unfold together…

the Red Sox are winning…bottom of the ninth.

*Stepping into the father's, the mother's, the son's, the daughter's,
the grandparent's, the best friend's, the lover's shoes for a moment—
what do you see differently…from their perspective? What starring
(or supporting) role can you play in rewriting the script for positive
change…for the best interest of the child or children?*

Two Veterans: Father and Son

BY REGINALD LOCKETT

The old man insists

on having his hair cut

only at the barbershop

at the base exchange

on Coast Guard Island.

His son who drives him there

once a month can't stand it.

He wants to be there

only as long as it takes

the blond white woman

to cut his father's hair

in the close military style

the old man has worn

since he enlisted in 1940.

If an appointment

isn't confirmed, it can be

two to three hours

of torture for the son,

but time to shop in the PX

or lunch in the mess hall

where the old man

can swap sea stories

with other old salts

who've found their way

to the last military base

near San Francisco.

The thirty-year Navy veteran,

who served in the Pacific

through World War II,

Korea, and Vietnam

loves to recall with other

old sailors, soldiers,

and marines shore leave

in Yokohama, Tokyo,

the Philippines, Hong Kong,

and San Diego.

An educator and artist, now,

the two-year draftee

only has chance encounters

with other Vietnam-era vets.

He's been back in the world

since his discharge

back in '69.

He hates any damn thing

that has to do with

the military.

No veterans hospital,

commissary, war movies,

Old Navy Stores where his kids

buy their clothes, nothing.

The old man is pushing

a well-earned ninety

and needs his help,

so he tolerates the sterility

and military stiffness

of the Coast Guardsmen

and the occasional

Navy Officer

who avoid staring directly

at this dread-locked denizen

of an industrial city's

catacombs of existence,

escorting his father

to this outpost on the edge

of Oakland.

The old man loves

the spit and polish

of these well-ordered places

and could never get used

to what the world outside

of those well-guarded gates

has to offer.

His son can't persuade him

to try Mr. C's Barbershop

or dine at Sweetie Pie's

or Lois's restaurants

right there in the city.

The way people, places,

and things change

leaves the old man

lost and confused.

Once the son watched

a French military ceremony

for the heroes of France's wars

at the Arc de Triomphe

and—strange of him—wished

his father there in Paris

with him at that moment.

The old man would've

really liked it and blessed

the dedication to France's

fallen heroes with

a polite salute.

There comes that season when the roles reverse. How can we be more to and do more for our elders?

Journey to Community Empowerment

My hands became tools to discern,
Magical in their abilities to feel what I could not see.
Instead of blind, dangling paws of acceptance,
Numb, heavy and best kept hidden in pockets.

—William Hobbs

Black to Basics

BY CURTIS V

Black man where is it you're coming from

Take the time black man learn how to raise not run

While you're out kickin it who's gonna raise your son

Let's face it get black to basics

Prepare yourself to fight to fight hard and long

Fight till you bleed or die to keep your family strong

Whenever you fight for what's right brother you never
    go wrong

Let's face it get black to basics

Who said that life was a breeze

    Because it's not do you freeze

Put your mind at ease

    No longer try to please

A failure takes his faults and tries to erase it,

    Let's face it black to basics

Babies making babies just to experience love

    Looking to gangs for strength when strength comes from
    above

Young mothers losing their childhood can never replace it

    Ignore the needs of the child, to go back to retrace it

It's a shame but there's nobody to blame

    Let's face it get black to basics

There ain't no family unity he loves her she loves him

    But when we see them out it's never we saw "them"

Nowhere to go for support nowhere for protection

    The first feeling you learn is the feeling of rejection

The recipe is clear I'm sure if you trace it

You'll see the need,

            To get BLACK TO BASICS

Getting black to basics, where shall I start…

A Call to Action

BY JAMES LEWIS

I grew tired of shaking my head.

It happened many times—while watching television, reading the paper, watching movies, combing through newsmagazines. Constant reminders pummeled my conscience, forcing me to face bell curves, so many statistics:

"One in three black males involved in the legal system…"

"Homicide: leading cause of death for black males…"

"Absentee fathers: 70 percent of black households headed by black women…"

"Despite growth in the economy, black males still lag behind…"

Every statistic seemed worse than the five years before. I saw no end.

At times, I wanted to scream. Other times, I felt embarrassed, especially around other races. The bad news stung. Each day, I had to don a new shield to combat the self-doubt, disgust, frustration and anger that swirled into one big cyclone of damaged emotion.

And always, always, I would shake my head.

As a black man, I limped under a dark cloud alongside other men "cursed" in skin like mine. No matter my status, no matter how much I wanted to hide the shame, those stats involved me, too. I couldn't run from the facts.

I felt like a prisoner handcuffed to a painful reality of low hope and rampant stereotyping. Get away from "them." They're thieves, rapists, drug dealers, murderers, HIV-carriers, downlowers, etcetera, etcetera. Propaganda always retold our story: *Black men remain several steps behind on the evolutionary ladder, destined to live at the bottom—of—the barrel with no chance of ascending. They are like un-neutered canines wreaking havoc on civility.*

And society wanted us there.

"Let 'em kill each other like savages!"

"Who cares about *them?*"

Well…at least, it seemed that way at times. Still does.

However, I didn't want to hear that mess. "Fed-up" became an understatement.

Tired of shaking my head, I wanted to do something.

What could one man do, though? How could I divert the crap poisoning young black minds? How could I show them that black men *do* give back?

Overcoming stats that exposed the plight of black men seemed as great a feat as climbing a rocky mountain with bare hands and feet. No excuses, though. I could do my part, so I chose to start climbing.

I figured, I didn't have to take on a crowd.

I could invest my energy in one person.

I became a Big Brother.

The only requirement was that I spend time with my little brother twice a month for a year, for at least three hours each time. Even with my military schedule, I knew I could and *would* commit. I wouldn't let the young man down.

During the interview, the representative shared another statistic that surprised me: Not only black boys, but boys in general, enrolled in Big Brothers Big Sisters would some-times stay on a waiting list for more than a year. Men, in general, weren't stepping up to the plate.

I decided not only to step up to the plate, but also to swing.

And, I specifically asked for a young African-American male.

After my evaluation and background check, I chose my little brother, an eight-year-old I'll call "Billy." Despite the forty-five-mile distance from my house, I signed on the dotted line. Twice a month, for at least three hours each time? The time commitment was a small investment for the potential of great rewards for both of us.

During the Big Brothers orientation, I met Billy, a shy yet personable young man who broke from his shell during a checkers game. We connected in no time.

Before I picked him up for our first getaway together, nervous jitters bit me.

How should I act?

What should we do?

Should I spend a lot of money to show him a good time?

I soon realized all I had to do was be his friend. And it was easy with a little brother who seemed ready to take on the world.

We did everything together—football, movies, amusement parks, car shows. I taught him a jump shot. He taught me Pokémon. We even went to a Prince concert.

He was *my* buddy, *my* little brother. His mother told me she'd noticed an immediate change in Billy. He seemed less withdrawn, more alive, more happy.

And I was, too. Our time together stirred the so-called "warm fuzzies" in me. It truly felt good.

But as they say, good times must end. Unfortunately, my military schedule became more demanding and after a year and a half, I had to drop from the program. Around the same time, Billy moved to another city.

In my eyes, Billy wouldn't become a "statistic." He was an ordinary kid who loved video games and often forgot to tie his tennis shoes. He was not a young man predetermined to fail because of his skin color. I did my best to show him that no matter what's said about us, brothas who care walk this earth.

When I retire from the military a few years from now, I plan to rejoin the Big Brothers program. Although Billy lives in another city, he will remain my little brother as long as I have life.

But I still have room for more…one little guy at a time.

And, which little (or not so little) guy will I be a Big Brother (or father) to? Here are three things that I will do to positively touch his life in his rite of passage to manhood…

an american like me

BY JIM MORENO

he lay motionless on mattress, like deadman, like noman, like American man. his tattered clothes, filthy clothes, american clothes cling to spiritlessness. at midday in LA. hearts lower to half mast, americans walk by this american— looking the other way…

she is distant, vacant, standing next to me. she is someone's grandma, american grandma, not the blue-eyed, rosy-cheeked, american grandma. she's the brown sparkling, spirited-eyed, fry bread, high red cheek-boned American grandma. one day she was navaho, next day she was no mind. now she asks me in downtown din for small change, any change that will buy her next drink. no lights are on. no one is home in this american home. american body selling, mind gone, american body selling to the lowest bidder as american heads turn the other way. american heads turning away from american grandma. american tears flow down, weeping rivers of remorse, rivers of sorrow for one more american lost.

american heads turn away from tears, american heads turn many ways, building theaters for warriors, entertainers, distracter gladiators with shoulder pads and face masks kicking tail so our town can go eleven and oh making heads turn, american heads turning away from no man, street sleeping, street dying, american heads turning away from american grandma selling herself for port wine, crackman smiling, paying politicians to look the other way.

american heads turn as ceo gulps his bonus from managed care cannibal corporations eating the sick, american sick, eating the old, american old, eating the insane, americans all, american heads turn as ceo rips his bonus after ripping jobs away from red, white, and blue workers, then giving those jobs to dark slave labor, dark child slaves far away, farther than minnesota, stockholders clutching two-car garage and the bottom line, no matter how many suffer, suffer from american greed.

american heads turn the other way not voting, american heads turn not choosing, american heads turning from fat-faced spin doctors secretly selling killing machines while openly pedaling war, spin doctors gobbling freedom, scarfing freedom, stealing freedom, without restraint, treason prospering by another name, treason against american people born free choosing to live unfree, choosing to give freedom away to racist neocon, pedagogues of subterfuge who claim to be patriots but are not concerned that the eagle flies free, only that the eagle flies on friday straight to only their nest and not yours, american agents of subterfuge, five-starred shadows murdering and doping the free for profit masked as freedom's flame,

killers selling killing machines, philistine power pedants gobbling freedom with industry of misery, building plethoras of prisons, money-making penitentiary factory gold-barred buildings exploiting, degrading, dehumanizing, american men, exploiting degrading, enslaving american women.

american men needing reborn fathers birthed in programs building paths away from poverty. american women needing mamas reborn in teaching the way to light. teachers lighting the walk away from darkness. american darkness, american shadows, american poverty of mind, american poverty of ideas, american shame of business of poverty, industry of suffering, industry of misery, industry of shame.

i weep for streetman. he stirs my heart, my american heart, my african heart, my asian heart, my european heart, my latino heart, my chicano heart, my native-american heart. motionless on his dirty mattress dying, his filthy death bed, breathing slows, labors, more american heads turn away...

don't turn away! don't turn your head! look into his eyes! american eyes! see noman, see streetman dying alone, shrinking freedom's song, your song, shredding the fabric of the flag of peace. there can be no peace, you can have no peace, i can have no peace if one streetman dies, one streetwoman dies alone.

you are too great for streetman to have nothing. you have so much to share for him to have only filthy death mat, you have too many gifts for her to have no home, you are too noble for her to die mindless...alone.

I look into navaho grandma's heart, american heart, I give her coins that will help her drink to death. she has to know she has a grandson, she has to know i am her grandson. she has to know. she has to know.

Sweet Dreams Are Made of This...

BY T. S. MURPHY

"Everybody's looking for something..." —*Eurythmics*

"Tell me what you want!" I yelled finally.

He gave me a slight gaze from light brown eyes that matched his complexion and were shaped like pecans. He sat up slightly from the chair that he had been stretched out in for the last thirty minutes of our educational counseling session and replied, "Well, my judge said that I have to get a GED while I'm in the program."

"Kevin," I said, "I know the judge is encouraging you to get a GED, but encouragement alone is not going to get you one."

Out of the participants that are referred to me for an educational assessment, fewer than half are GED-ready, one-fourth of them are not able to spell GED.

"I know, Murphy, I know…ah right, I wanna play ball for the Knicks and have a honey like J.Lo on my arm." He laughed and threw back his head.

Kevin had what some black folks call "good hair." It was corn rowed back into two long braids that dangled as he laughed.

"I'm not laughing, Kevin. This isn't a joke."

But in many ways, it was a joke. Kevin was sent to this program for a felony charge of drug possession. If he completed the six months with us, he would get five years' probation. Kevin was just like most of the brothers I have worked with for more than ten years. They had dropped out of school way before they dropped into the penal system. This lanky, seventeen-year-old charmer in front of me had not been in school for three years.

"Yo, could you believe they threw me out of school because they caught me and some girl on the staircase? I was on lunch." He later added, "So forget 'em, I never went back."

Yeah, I thought. You showed them.

"Kevin, I'm going to enroll you in our Adult Basic Education class."

"Why… C'mon, black man!"

"The Judge wants you involved in some form of education process," I said. "You're seventeen, no high school credit, and no job. You c'mon!"

"Yo," he leaned back again into his perfect smile. "I had a job…it was just off the books."

"It's your 'job,'" I said, "that got you here."

"Yo, I was just tryin' to represent, you know."

It's that representing, I thought, that landed your behind right in this program.

After the first couple of weeks in class, Kevin adjusted better than most of the participants in the program. He was the first one I saw in the morning as I came in the door, tired, with a cup of Colombian coffee, the cup that helps me to do what was put before me every morning—teach young people to build better tomorrows.

He was stretched out on a bench, half asleep.

"Why are you here so early? Class doesn't start until 10:30."

"Yo, I'm just tryin' to do what I got to do to get up out of this program."

Many mornings later, he would tell me why he was there so early. His thirty-something mother had a twenty-something boyfriend who didn't want her seventeen-year-old son "laying around, eating the stuff" he bought. So before the boyfriend got up in the morning, Kevin would leave and come lie on the bench, waiting for the cup of Colombian that I would occasionally bring him.

When I took this job, I came armed with the "each one, teach one" philosophy. I was going to enlighten every young black male that came into my classroom. I wanted to save them, from the streets, the drugs and each other. The courts, on the other hand, wanted them to be monitored, to be kept off the streets and not to be involved in any "illegal acts."

They would say, "I want you to get a GED while you're in this program," but in reality, it was close to impossible. Kevin and the other young men I was instructed to "monitor and teach some basic skills" had dropped out of school. They came into the program with a second-grade reading level and a math level that only makes sense on some street corner. They were supposed to be able to earn a GED by the time they graduated the six-month program and I only had them in my class for four. Kevin's dream made more sense. It would be easier to get into the NBA.

All of these young men wanted what Kevin wanted—to do the time they were sentenced to and get out of the program. Now, if that meant going to class and listening to me go on and on about the importance of education, so be it. They would do whatever it took to keep themselves in the streets, nightclubs or bed of some young girl. Most, if not all, didn't believe in education.

Over coffee in the mornings and in class in the afternoons, I saw in Kevin what I saw in some of the other brothers—a ray of hope, a flicker of thought, a sign that there was something more than the gold he wore and the designer clothes he bragged about getting from older women that made him feel wanted.

Kevin was one of the few who would ask why. "Why we got to write an essay? Why we got to read this boring story? Why we got to go to the museum?"

After whining like a baby, he would do his work and participate.

Most of the brothers would not say or do anything. They would just sit there, going through the motions. The mere fact that I said something and Kevin had a comment and opinion, showed me there were signs of potential in him. Outside of class, I was the one asking why.

"Why didn't you finish school? You are quite bright. Why did you sell drugs? There are other ways of making money that will keep you out of jail. Why don't you finish this assignment? I know you can."

After a while it became a game between the two of us:

"Why, Murphy, Why?"

"Why not, Kevin?" I replied. "Why not?"

We would talk about the problems he had with his mother, his girls and his life overall.

"It be stressin' me, Murphy."

"You make choices that are stressin' you. Make better choices."

Part of my job was to help them identify what they are looking for.

"I don't think that J.Lo dates men without GEDs," I'd joke. "You can't get into the NBA if you can't read the contract."

In the months to come, Kevin got into a GED program and a part-time job, although part of me believes that he did it more for me than himself.

"Yo, Murphy," he would say from his morning bench in the hallway. "I expect a large Colombian for getting into school."

I looked to show the courts and maybe the world that we couldn't throw away young, black men—my attempt at "revolutionary recycling." I wanted to give these brothers a fighting chance in a seemingly losing battle. Kevin had become my latest weapon and part of my dream. He was my Stevens (who was killed in gang battle), my Roberts (who was killed in a stolen-car chase) and my Watson (who left the program early one day to commit a homicide, and was sentenced to fifteen years). If Kevin could make it through, those sweet dreams wouldn't be in vain.

The last time I saw Kevin, he was coming for a monitoring with his case manager. He was in school, and according to him, trying to live right.

"Murph, I had to let that older honey go," he said "She be trying to tell me I can't make it in school. I can't go by my old corner too much. Brothers want you to hang out, but I'll lose my job if I don't get up on time.

"My mom's still trippin', but I'm seeing if I can get a room somewhere until I get on my feet."

"You are standing on your feet," I said. "You just have to keep walking in the right direction."

Kevin walked in the opposite direction one early April morning, as I was getting ready to plant more sweet dreams into young minds. The direction he went, according to the report filed weeks later, was into a neighborhood club and into the arms of some gang member's woman. He was standing on his feet when a gunshot tore into his pretty-boy head. He was probably dead before he reached the floor.

The courts wanted them "placed." I wanted them to dream. And they wanted everything they *thought* would make them into men. In imparting dreams to my students, I didn't tell them that bullets kill dreams and dreamers. They already knew the realities of how they lived. Maybe that's why they didn't dream. Maybe I should have been taking a lesson from them. How many lives did I have to see lost to realize the goal was not getting a GED but staying alive.

I used to walk by that bench, with my Colombian, hoping it would be occupied by someone with a flicker of whys. I would drink my coffee, get ready for my next assessment, my next class, my next...I tried to forget. Just as I tried to forget Stevens, Roberts, Watson and others who I thought could escape this vicious cycle through education and some direction.

The only thing I could do was leave my door open for the next Q and A's of "What do you want?"

Honestly, I don't know the answers anymore.

Simple Words That Shaped

BY WIL CASON

The fabric of the family is woven with so many moments of excitement and of sorrow.

With thirty minutes to spare before boarding the airplane to Tampa, I called my brother-in-law, Lawrence, to give him my travel itinerary. Lawrence suggested calling my dad's hospital room to let him know I was coming to visit. The nurse on duty answered the phone. Lawrence told her that Mr. Cason's youngest son was on the phone and wanted to speak with him.

The nurse responded with a slight quiver in her voice, "I am sorry to inform you this way, but Mr. Cason 'expired' thirty minutes ago."

Tears filled my eyes and numbness fell on my heart as I boarded the plane. I prepared for a long trip.

You can never anticipate what will lead you to reflect on the true meaning of family until life happens. As I drove to the airport that morning to catch a plane from California to Florida, I began reflecting on the wonderful conversations and lessons of life I learned from my father.

As a child, spending the day with my dad was exciting. One Saturday, I was waiting for him to take me to work with him. Hearing the sound of the eighteen-wheeler and seeing the brown truck driving down the road would elate any child. We spent the day delivering freight throughout central Florida.

"Have respect for yourself and treat others with respect," he said.

At sixteen, I rode with my dad in his sky blue, stretch Cadillac as we talked about life. His words resounded, "Son, whatever you do in life, be the best you can be." As a child, his powerful words were deposited into my heart. They were simple yet meaningful. They helped me to take tasks and challenges head-on throughout my life.

"Son, be the best you can be."

The foundation of the family and community is love, and the loving voices of the family and community speak to the hearts of every individual. Those voices challenge us to live a life that transports hopes, dreams, possibilities and visions from one generation to the next. My mother's voice was gentle.

"A good name is more powerful than education or money," she said.

Voices from family and community awaken potential in the lives of children.

"Do things that will make your family and community thankful."

Walking past Ms. Annie Lee's house, I'd hear inspiring words:

"You are going to make it, Willie Love."

"Obey your parents."

"Don't follow the crowd."

"I'm proud of you, Willie Love."

Ms. Annie Lee always called me Willie Love because she saw me as a lovable person. Those simple words from Ms. Annie Lee and other neighbors have inspired me to give hopeful, healing and harmonious affirmations to my children and others I meet as a motivational speaker.

As a father, I know how vital words are when communicating to my children. I know the tremendous impact of my words in my sons' lives. On the drive to preschool is a good time for us to talk. I see them beam when I tell them that they are kings, brilliant and wonderful. We talk a lot on the twenty-minute ride to school. I ask what they like best about school, their friends, likes and dislikes, and what they look forward to doing that day. I give them positive and powerful words to start their day.

My desire is to build loving and trusting relationships with my children by communicating with them daily.

"I am thankful that I am your father and you are my sons—you both are the best."

Nurturing words release you to expand and create a greater personal vision. When life has presented me with a moving experience, I have replayed that moment many times over with my family, my community and my sons. From the cab of that big rig, his voice continues to ring in my ear.

"Be the best you can be, son."

With the words we speak to our children, families and communities, we can open up a future of great possibilities.

A few days ago, I asked my four-year-old son, "What do you think I mean when I say be the best you can be?"

"Be a leader."

"Great. And, you are a leader, son."

Today, I will pick up the phone, send an e-mail, write a note or speak face-to-face to someone who needs to hear loving, encouraging words from me.

Set Me Free

BY BRENTON ROLLE

In order for you to break free of something, you must first recognize that you are being held or restricted by it. We as black people are often caught in a sea of poverty and debt and we sometimes don't even know it. The enslavement isn't just in our wallets, but also in our minds. We have been conditioned, in many cases, by those who love us the most, that we should go out and get a good job, work for thirty or forty years at that job and then retire. Sadly, however, retirement means accepting a meager pension from someplace at two-thirds of what we used to earn, if we're lucky. Even worse is having no pension or retirement plan in place and an even less adequate social security check.

In order to grasp the scope of the enslavement of our minds, we must understand and accept several basic premises that will lead us to a greater understanding of how to get out of debt.

First, we must accept that working for an hourly wage is the least advantageous, least efficient way of accumulating money. For a minimum of eight hours a day, five days a week, we must report to a place of business and accept a wage someone else thinks that we should have. People argue that their work is undervalued and that they aren't being paid what they are worth; however, they continue to report to that job and accept that wage. So, in effect, we make the conscious or unconscious decision that our time is worth exactly what the wage per hour says we're worth. The fact that you don't determine that wage is exactly what makes it enslavement. *Most people haven't given consideration to the flow of the money that is generated by their hard work. We only focus on the hourly wage or salary.*

Second, most people have an "employee" mind-set. We're willing and conditioned to respect our jobs first and ourselves and our families second. If you don't believe me then total the number of hours you spent last week at your job, and then calculate the number of hours you spent with your family. Go ahead and include the weekend. That won't make the ratio much better for many people.

John D. Rockefeller said that he would rather have one percent of the efforts of one hundred men than one hundred percent of his own. That's why companies are designed for CEOs and shareholders to get rich.

Finally, we have to change our thinking so that we can set ourselves free by understanding the concept of *passive* income. Passive income is money generated by a source that is constantly in motion, bringing in resources without the recipient having to report to a job. Even owning your own business can be, in some cases, more stressful than working for someone else. If you are spending all of your time and efforts working on your own, and only making wages by the amount of hours that you put in, then you have still missed the concept of passive income.

We must develop a product, system or idea that can generate income without the direct trade of hours for dollars. Owning income-producing property is one way of developing passive income. If you own five apartments and each has a mortgage of one hundred thousands dollars, and you had to make a monthly mortgage payment of five hundred dollars per apartment, you would then have a payout of twenty-five hundred dollars per month. If each of those apartments were rented for eight hundred and fifty dollars per month, you would have an income of more that four thousand dollars each month. By applying simple mathematics, your net income would then be close to two thousand dollars per month. Although you would have to manage the property and its upkeep, the best part is that your income would be the same whether you went to work that day or not. You could be next door or five thousand miles away, and your income would remain the same. This is just one form of passive income. There are also royalties from original books, movies and screenplays; residual income from network marketing businesses; income from coin-operated machines and so on.

The greatest discovery is the realization of our own potential. The secret to extraordinary achievement is exploiting your unknown potential.

So you say you want to be free? Do your homework. Invest in your personal, spiritual and financial education and *learn* how to set yourself free.

Here are three action steps I'm taking to better manage my money and/or to make more/save more/invest more money to set myself and my family free....

Love Notes

You walk through my dreams
I hear the language of jazz
Feel the pulse of stars

—Reginald Lockett

R.S.V.P.

BY CURTIS V

I wonder if what I saw when I was looking at you

Was the same sensuous scene that turns me on like you do

Your sexy eyes looking at me made me feel like a king

But that was just a look you see because the body, the body
didn't have to do a thing

Oh but when you moved the body I got the message that
it sent

That's when we connected and all of your inhibitions went

We're standing face-to-face do you want a kiss and I know
I can

But to enhance this kiss I'll start with the touch of a slow
    hand

So methodically moving to all of your sensual, erogenous
    spots

Now inside and out you experience your whole body
    getting hot

So hot if it were measured the mercury would bust the gage

Melting the lock, unleashing the sexual beast from its cage

And your body movement was like a written invitation
    to me

And my body, my body only R.S.V.P.'d

You Make Me Poetry

BY H. L. NICHOLS

Baby you make

Me poetry

As I find myself

Fiending to find myself

The divine in your caramel

Complexion perfection

Double dipped in dimple

Perfect, classic beauty, no pimple

I perspire cause there's fire

In them eyes, best believe

Just blessed I can't lie

Baby you make

Me poetry

And I've been mesmerized

Enthralled, on the real confused

Cause I don't know what to

I can't get over

If you find the words let me know too cause

Baby you make

Me poetry

For 38 years plus two

I've journeyed simply to find

Love like yours, Love like you

Open my eyes to see

Love was never blind

Can't get you off

My mind cause

Baby you make

Me poetry

And like right now

So Beautiful I can't breathe

Cause I ain't ready

To believe that one

Such as you would ever come

Not my way, not today

The dream I couldn't conceive cause

Baby you make

Me poetry

Ahhh…umm…

You make me

Poetry

And I Said

BY CURTIS V

She said to come and sit, I'm sure you'd rather not stand

It's hard for me to say this in a way that you'll even understand

She said it's not you, it's me, because you know you're a
hell of a man

But I need my space to find me and I don't see you in that
plan

And I said this is something that I always knew

And I said that's why the relationship never grew

And I said you'll never recognize the good that I do

And I know that we're through so I'll leave you to be you

Now that we're being true to ourselves, let's put it all on the line

Let's end this on a friendship tip, You go your way and THANKS I'll go mine

There's no need for you to feel trapped, who knows what treasures you may find

Make sure whoever it is they love you as much as who you've left behind

And I said this is something that I always knew

And I said that's why the relationship never grew

And I said you'll never recognize the good that I do

And I know that we're through so I'll leave you to be you

I ain't mad at you you've obviously got problems unresolved

Take the time to know you and that's one problem that you'll solve

If you know who you are, your feelings are secure and won't ever dissolve

And the person lying next to you, you'll love and never feel appalled

And I said this is something that I always knew

And I said that's why the relationship never grew

And I said you'll never recognize the good that I do

And I know that we're through so I'll leave you to be you

She said it's not that I don't want to be your friend just not your wife

I think it would be better for the both of us to go out and start a new life

She said I didn't know how to tell you this feeling this way

Unbeknownst to her when you're unloved to hear it's over is like INDEPENDENCE DAY

And I said thanks for the time you've given me

And I said no longer unloved now I'm free

And I said now I can shine for someone else to see

You're no longer stuck with me,

And we're both set free

INDEPENDENCE DAY

Independence Day...the Remix

BY MARIA DOWD-VENTERS

Your Independence Day was my thanks giving,

That fateful day when we really started living.

No fireworks, though, on that blessed night,

Only azure sky, music and gentle moonlight.

No windows of distractions to our mutual attraction

But, the door did swing open and I peeked in,

Just an innocent look, nothing to defend

At the time, I didn't know who you were,

But knew your tempo bumped with my swerve.

I saw that bent smile and those smooth dance grooves,

Your slender hips calling forth my every move.

We shared that dance, just you and me.

Unbeknownst to us, it was our first ride to eternity.

God commanded this mating call,

Curtis V and Maria D overheard it all.

Your Independence Day was my thanks giving.

That fateful day when we really started living.

Give love an infusion of that stuff that makes her smile, laugh, cry, love you all over again. Today (and for many days to come), for _____, I'll...

A Renegade Woman

BY JIHMYE COLLINS

When she comes into view,

i want to have to fasten

my seat belt

each step toward me

earth trembling under foot,

sounds of a soft bass symphony

her voice a clap of muffled thunder

in the face

of an unjust deed,

but ticklishly soothing

over the lobe of my devilishly desiring ear

i want a renegade woman

a renegade woman

appreciating differences,

seeing color, relishing in it

acknowledging and understanding privilege

and the inequity of it

renegade woman

a radical for the common man

and woman, who will advocate

for sending no more sons

or daughters to combat hostilities

soothing the eager itch of war-makers

a woman of tenderness

and grit

a fondness for baubles,

but caring less about baubles

and things,

more of nature walks,

sunsets over the Pacific,

a steaming cup of passion fruit tea,

or Kenya AA java,

at a quaint neighborhood shop

no Starbucks chi-chang, frappe, frosty, fluffy,

   fruit-fritz

a renegade woman

conscious, standing tall for equality,

wearing long pants

with men of integrity,

who'll also allow me to open her door,

or let me be on top—

sometimes

renegade woman

no fear of wearing a cocked hat

over one eye,

styling,

or fixin' a drip drip

under the kitchen sink,

almost professionally,

which is outta my league,

but lovingly nurturing and loving

loving, like only a woman can

renegade woman

a maestro with recipes

smoked pheasant under glass, escargot, bouillabaisse,

or collard greens, black-eyed peas

and fried to the bone cat fish

renegade woman

a quilted knowledge

of world affairs, community and service

service to humanity,

swirling in a lust for justice

with a Sheehan armor

yet soothing me

with lyrics that beckon

a jitney ride

on a silent moonbeam,

fulfilling that ultimate dream

with my renegade woman

Describe the renegade woman in your world, the renegade woman who makes your head swirl...

The Blooming

BY WILLIAM B. T. TAYLOR

A seed of light is planted in the dark crevice of your broken heart.

Your pain feels unbearable. The anguish that has overtaken you feels devastating.

As your heart continues to break, the seed breaks open.

Becoming a radiant flower glowing in the darkness.

Be very careful not to close your heart,

or the joyful flower of pure love will not bloom.

If there is any pain that can be released forever, now is time to let it go…

And Their Hearts Beat On

BY MARIA D. DOWD

As I sit here in one-at-every-corner coffee shop, editing and writing, opening and closing files, seeking the *himvoices* that sing songs to my heart, I overhear the folks at the counter, mostly young female voices, still raving about their mad love for the movie *The Five Heartbeats*. My mind smiles, as I think about my firstborn's millionth rewind, she, too, hooked on the story of these five young bloods. My baby girl hates that term, as it means something so different to the younger generation. To me, it's endearing, like a motherly hug. So you have these *young bloods* getting their groove on, succumbing and triumphing, again and again… to the fifth power. Then there is that mad love…at the end of the day, found, saved, loved, respected, at ease in their gray-templed, be-speckled lives at the backyard barbecue, whooping that doo-wop like yesterday was just yesterday.

I look over the top of my laptop and a *young blood* is sitting across from me, *sportin'* (Is this term okay, my beloved daughters?) his grill like the Holy Grail. Of course, I want to ask, *why,* but I trust that it's just another youthful phase, like the plaid undershorts that my be-spectacled eyes—oops—just saw too much of. Forgive the sidebar, but these kids kill me with their adornments. Lots of Laughs, Laugh Out Loud, (LOL), *whatever.* Back to my laptop.

The storyline…

…five hearts beating for one another with mad dreams of making it big…every man's dream…of making it big so he can stand onstage (usually with his *homies*…I trust that this term is still used), holding that mic sideways, thanking God first, and then mama; or mama first, and then God. And either is okay with the world. Sometimes pops is in the mix, and sometimes not. Not sure if that's so okay with the world, but it is what it is. Nonetheless, crunched on the top of his sneakers and tucked under his sideways-worn cap with the tag dangling on top, the hopes and dreams for bling-bling, beemers and bread for mama…but this time around only the very best, imported whole grains, offered up in a custom-designed twenty-four-carat gold, straight from South Africa diamond-studded bread basket. No more water-insoluble dollar loaves of bread off of the week-old shelf from the corner market.

Why did this movie make such an impression on our then teenage daughters? Okay, The Heartbeats were cute, each in his unique cuddly, nerdy, sexy, womanizing, zealous, naive, ambitious, gifted way. But is there something more that keeps our now twenty-fivish-year-old daughters talking about it. I stopped writing for a moment to reach out to one of the founding fan club members, my firstborn. I called her at work, and she promised to e-mail her answer to my question, "What do you love most about the movie?" While I await her answer, I'll quickly share that two other women and I, a while back, did a tribute to The Five Heartbeats. Three beats showed for the film and talk in my home-town—the main dude with the vision and direction, along with the reddish one and the tall guy, who dons a first name only. I'm sure his mama and daddy gave him two, but the one works. Yep, it sure does. Hummm, might there be a Five Heartbeats fiftyish mamas fan club?

Okay, back to the storyline. My opinion is that the movie takes us on that roller coaster of reaching for the top, flound-ering, rebounding, finding God, our calling, love, family and happiness. On the fifth beat, the camera reels us (click, click, click of the heels)…back home, to the backyard, where the tradition prevails. This is what most little girls and grown women want, despite our sometimes-antsy attitudes, lofty qualifiers and desperate acts of all kinds of foolishness. And, this is what most little boys and grown men want, despite the same. None of us is off the hook. The reality is too many of us (and I'm not excluding myself) have worked way too hard on not making it work, and our little girls and little boys are left with few choices but to live vicariously through the scenes on the big screen…and at the mercy of the big-screen filmmakers. *Oh, Lord.*

Thank you, Robert, for giving our young sisters some hope to hold on to, and things still worthy of talking about some fifteen years after the movie's making, where the young women were depicted in real, yet positive, supporting roles.

And, their hearts beat on.

Pull out that old video (if you still own it) or DVD, pop some corn and watch a favorite "love" story with a dear one, and describe what is reawakened in the two of you….

Tenderness

BY ERIC W. SMITH

Come here, baby

You don't have to hurt to love me

It's not about the pain you can bear

Your daddy did you wrong as a baby

Somebody always had to touch you there

You lay awake at night crying

You hear the sounds of, "Don't! Please stop!" fill the air

When morning comes you know she'll be denying

That he beat her down with the kitchen chair

Let me heal your bitterness

With a little tenderness

Let me hold you

I won't hurt you

The love I give is gonna last

I'll help you through your painful past

Let me love you

And we'll make all your dreams come true

The nightmares make you toss and turn

Your innocence has been snatched away

The smell, the taste, the ashes burn

The alcohol has stolen another day

So now you ask the Lord for His direction

And you pray for love and romance

But what you feel is His rejection

But, I'm your knight, baby, give me a chance

You try to love, but you've seen too much

I try to give, but you just can't trust

Give us a chance; let's try together

Let God build a love that lasts forever, Oh

Let me love you (Let me love you)

Let God love you (Don't give up on God, He's got a plan
   for you)

Let you love you (So just stand up tall, and hold your head
   up high)

And you'll see all your dreams come true.

Love Is Coming at You...
Twice the Speed of Lightning

BY JEFFERY MENZISE

I've got this friend...no, really, a good friend of mine that grew up in the inner city of Cincinnati, Ohio, with his mother, grandmother and older sister in the household. Yup, the all-too-common black male experience—no consistent, strong, loving, caring examples of black manhood or black loving relationships between a man and woman, more specifically between a husband and a wife.

Fast-forwarding into the future, bypassing years of superficial relationships with females and many tense and short-lived interactions with male "friends," my good friend narrowly escaped the fate of many of his drug-dealing peers, his drug-addicted male family members and his non–child-support-payment-making associates.

He had many angels in his life, including one named Angela (no kidding), who presented my friend with an application to a historically black university. My friend was accepted and prepared for his move. His mother and aunt, along with his little cousins, piled into his grandmother's car and headed south. It was during his college days that my friend learned of his pain and anger toward his father and the resulting conflicts with other males. It is here that he realized that he has always wanted better for his mother and his sister, so he would, in turn, attempt to be better *by* them and other females in his life…however consistent or inconsistent (this depends on who you ask).

The one true ladylove of his life made her transition, leaving my friend to pose hard questions to God. On many nights he sat in the chapel crying, wishing that he would have returned home to help ease his grandmother's passing into the realm of the ancestors. He prayed for guidance, correct living, strength and, above all, he prayed for wisdom, as King Solomon had in the Holy Bible.

During his days at the university, my friend found greater understanding, greater wisdom, through ancient African philosophical studies. Through this refinement, my friend met another angel on his path. She came in the form of a godmother. Over salmon biscuits, she spoke to him about Sufism and spirituality. Godmother had recently read a book on this spiritual practice rooted in Islam. She wondered if he knew anything of it. At this point he hadn't heard of it but would look into it.

Although he never "became" a Sufi (neither did his godmother), his godmother provided the type of transgenerational conversation that is missing from the lives of too many of our children, and she began to chip away at that hardened portion of my friend's heart that rarely heard the words "I love you" come from a caregiver, a loved one, a family member or himself. She would end every phone conversation with those magical words and the concept that they represent. He would just say "okay" and get off the phone.

She eventually confronted him. "Why don't you ever say 'I love you, too'?" He was floored. He felt uneasy with the feelings and the memories, or the lack thereof, indicating that he was neither used to hearing the words nor saying them. What did this mean? Was this fact indicative of his mother's lack of love for him? Was it indicative of the lack of love throughout his life? No. Of course not. But it wasn't so clear to him. He slowly processed these experiences and questions and eventually began to say "I love you, too." Another hurdle jumped…but wait, another one was coming up fast.

Now that he was armed with four words and the courage to verbalize them, he was well on his way to emotional healing. After months of practice saying "I love you, too," my friend was faced with the next challenge, truly an opportunity to reconcile some pain and bring about healing—he pared four words down to three. He tried dropping the word "I" but that wasn't it. Then he tried to drop the word "love," but that defeated the purpose. He then attempted by removing the word "you," which wasn't bad but still not quite right. Of course, the hardest word to drop was "too," which meant that he would have to begin to verbalize his feelings not only as a response but as the initiator.

Where would he begin? If you guessed with his mother, then you must know the story. He made the tough decision to begin saying "I love you" to his mother at the end of their phone conversations. He recalled the fear of knowing what he was going to do at the end of their conversation. For once, he was not so quick to get off the phone. He sat and listened and conversed with his mother around any and everything, just as long as the conversation did not end. After he had prolonged the conversation as long as humanly possible, he finally sneezed out the words "I love you."

It caught her by surprise. She was now confronted with her "stuff." What had happened to her son to allow him the freedom to express this to her? How dare he make her deal with her feelings openly. He has some nerve.

"I love you, too."

That wasn't so bad, right? It soon spread to his brother and sister, other loved ones, especially elders…and to children who surely needed to hear and feel the words.

Another hurdle jumped. However, what was that ahead? Yup, you guessed it, another hurdle.

Now my friend has graduated, twice, first with a bachelor's in psychology, and second with a master's in clinical psychology. He is on his way to the Mecca, to Chocolate City, from down south to up south, to Washington, D.C., to pursue his doctorate. However, during the summer before his move, my friend received a communication from a good friend, former housemate and home girl from Cincinnati. She shared that she'd prayed to God while sitting in a refugee camp in Tanzania, East Africa. She asked God to reveal who her soul mate and future husband was. She told him that God revealed that it was to be my friend. Can you imagine? These were two individuals who'd lived in the same neighborhood in Cincinnati, six streets apart, and never knew each other.

Prior to this revelation, she'd heard tales of my friend. She was on her way to Tennessee and was advised to look him up when she arrived. Well, she found him. Then she transferred to the university he was attending that next year, and majored in psychology as well. They weren't good friends at first. They just hung out from time to time. They eventually became closer while on a trip to Ghana together. Subsequently, they shared a house—she lived upstairs, he lived downstairs—strictly platonic for about two months before she graduated and went to the District of Columbia to pursue her master's. It was some time later when she disclosed this message from God. My friend didn't think too long about it. He simply said, "Okay."

When she returned from Africa, they became a couple. And, after many trials and tribulations, they realized that neither of them had sufficient nor effective models of black love. Sure, they were both well educated and had traveled extensively. However, neither knew the first thing about having a healthy relationship. They endured, she more than he at times. While they attempted to salvage the relationship, they realized that much of their current problems were a result of the absence of manhood and black love in their respective homes. Additionally, he didn't feel as though his mother loved him, and she didn't feel nurtured by her father—hence the potential of that generational curse called "The Crumbling Black Family."

"We are better than this," they declared. They agreed to suffer through the hard times and find resolution. After all, she'd made it out of the projects, and he off the block. Both had two degrees in social service-related fields. However, they came to realize that their training often excluded the substance and cultural competence in relation to the black experience, their experience. After an immeasurable amount of self-work, the two were beginning to see what was necessary to bring about healing. They worked on becoming friends, in addition to being husband and wife. This hurdle was cleared.

But wait. Need I say it…here came another.

Now capable of learning to love each other and healing their past traumas, disappointment and displaced expectations, God thought it would be cool to see how they would fare with a child. And, with the assistance of spiritual priests and priestesses and an angel in the form of a midwife, the couple prepared for the blessed arrival. At the birth center and throughout the labor, they danced to African drumming and chanted to Shango between cool showers, walks around the neighborhood, vitamins and red raspberry–based homeopathic concoctions. On that Friday night, a single flash of lightning and one deeply felt crackle of thunder announced the crowning of their son's head, the ring of fire. Maternal Granny was on her way from the train station and paternal Granny was strategically trying to get time off from work without losing her job. The couple's healthy baby uttered some words in the ancient language that many arrogantly dismiss as "baby talk."

Was this the final hurdle? Was this my friend's chance to cross the finish line and begin to live life on the right side of love? Probably not. However, he did feel love, and was now capable of showing it, in most situations, without hesitation. He is now able to look back over life and see all of the examples of sacrifice and loving actions displayed by his mother in her own way. She never let them starve, she kept shelter over their heads, she worked hard and sacrificed tremendously to send her children to better schools. That's LOVE!

My friend readily acknowledges that insecurity played a major part in his reservations about expressing his feelings. He realizes that so many of his issues with love stemmed from lack of support and tangible experiences with his own father. He also acknowledges that his difficult time with love equally stemmed from his mother's own hardships as a single parent. Now it's clear to him that if we, as adults, do not openly share our love for each other and our children, our children will be faced with similar dilemmas and hardships.

Let's begin to heal ourselves from within and shine our

light on each other and our children. Oh, yeah, and learn how to be a friend to yourself. It makes the journey that much more enjoyable and provides a safe space to tell one's life story.

Tell someone, "I love you," today....

Beneath the Bridge

BY CURTIS V

In the sun is where they sat beneath the bridge, staring out above the rail

As they watched each other's light brown skin turn to bronze from slightly pale

One shared a thought the other a feeling and both a little bit of humor

Being oh so careful all the while not to start the slightest rumor

They walked along the waterfront at first it seemed with little meaning

Until the moment became much more intense as the sun
continued beaming

Their eyes met once then again and then became a gaze

As they suddenly found themselves amid a definite but
pleasant haze

Although this space was different they enjoyed it all the
while

And to capture this special moment they stole a kiss then a
smile

Ooh it felt so good they wished it could last forever but of
course no way

Would father time allow that to happen as he began the
closing of his day?

Now they've captured and sealed this moment now this
feeling will always be there

As that warm feeling is the only thing to help them weather
the now dampened air

Nightfall has come and with it a chill like that out of a fridge

But what a wonderful day they shared when they sat in the
sun beneath the bridge.

Just Friends

BY H. L. NICHOLS

I get lost in your eyes,

Your smile sets you apart,

Your body beckons me to sin,

But we're just friends,

Don't want to lose,

Lose you my friend,

Realizing that my dreams would make us lovers,

Bed partners I have known if only for the night,

One night stands…listless affairs,

In avoidance of true love,

Every moment that you were not there,

What you know of me,

I know so much about you,

Intimate thoughts we share,

Expressions of how deeply we care,

You with me…set my soul free,

I pray this love…will forever be,

Because you are my friend,

We just happened to fall in love.

"Just friends," lovers, husbands and wives…ask yourself if you are living with integrity. If not, how can you change that?

A West Philadelphia Love Story

BY ERIC DOUGLASS JOHNSON

This tale begins in West Philadelphia, circa 1992, maybe '63. Like most African-American children of that era, I was forced to play outdoors for hours...in the summer heat. In those days, mothers didn't allow their children to play indoors unless it was raining fire, or stray cats and dogs were dropping dead in the street. There was never a good reason for a child to be in the house on a summer day. It could be a thousand degrees outside but it was always hotter down south where somebody's momma grew up.

"It ain't that hot out there," my mother would say. "You children don't know hot. It was so hot in Alabama that the mule had to wear sunglasses so his eyes wouldn't boil out of his head."

You had to stay outside until your mother called you. And, when she called, you had to go home immediately. Most kids knew not to make the woman of the house call them twice, and it was unheard of for kids to make their mothers come and get them. I don't remember what most of the mothers in my neighborhood looked like. You never actually saw these women, you just heard their voices.

To survive the hot days, we played games: Dumb School, Freeze Tag, Red Light/Green Light, and my personal favorite, Hot Cold Butter Bean, which was basically a ghetto version of Hide-and-Seek.

After a day of running, chanting, jumping, hiding and seeking, we worked up a *huge* thirst—not an ordinary thirst, but an "open your mouth and dust flies out" kind of thirst. Kids learned early not to ask to come in the house for a drink. Mothers back then were shrewd. Allowing a drink would only cause kids to have to use the bathroom, and using the bathroom was the king of all childhood plots to get back into the house. So most of us walked the streets blinded by thirst, dreaming of Kool-Aid.

There was, however, one oasis available only to children blessed to live near the corner of Haverford Avenue and Thompson Street. On that corner stood a police station that housed an old marble water fountain that served up the coldest, sweetest water on earth. My cousin lived just down the street from the station so I spent many a summer day ripping and running up and down Thompson Street, secure in the knowledge that I could quench my thirst.

I remember once lining up at the fountain behind a little girl. Like the rest of us kids, she panted and slurped at the fountain's cool liquid. However, there was something different about this girl. She was petite, golden brown and had two long twisted plaits of hair gathered at the ends with bright red barrettes. Normally, I would have done what boys do—rudely push her out of the way so that I could get my slurp on. But she smelled sweet, like a birthday cake layered with vanilla icing. And, even though she was missing most of her teeth, her smile lit up the dingy confines of the precinct.

Perhaps it was her beauty or delirium brought on by the ninety-degree heat wave that let my grimy little brown hand touch hers as she twisted the water faucet. She looked up at me with one of those "you better get your grubby little hand offa me" looks that boys find irresistible. I stared down at her, and she looked back up at me with a shy, toothless seven-year-old grin. It was love at first sight as I stood there staring at her through a pair of thick glasses mashed crookedly on my sweaty face.

Day after day, I lined up at that fountain looking for the little tan girl with the plaits, but she never showed up again.

I began thinking that maybe I had just imagined the whole thing.

Years passed, and like most young brothers, I forgot about my first brush with love. Now a college sophomore, I was *definitely* interested in women, but not necessarily love. While checking out the freshmen crop of sisters, I saw a young coed sitting in the cafeteria. She was cute, serious, sensible, quiet and kind. In other words, she was everything that I wasn't. This naturally made her even more irresistible. She wore her hair in a different style every day: the curly Afro, Afro puffs, ponytails, with each style more intriguing than the last.

It took weeks before I worked up the courage to talk to her. I mean *really* talk to her in the way that brothers "rap" when they *really* like a woman. I decided to make my move at a party being hosted in my dormitory. The party was hot and funky, which was considered a good thing. After years of playing outside in oppressive heat as a kid, most black students not only tolerated, but enjoyed the heat and the funk.

Finally, I garnered the nerve to ask if I could walk her back to her dormitory across campus. I didn't say much. I didn't say anything. Finally she started talking, and it turned out that the pretty coed was from Philly.

As we walked, I felt drawn to let my hand fall next to hers.

She took it, squeezed it playfully, looked up at me and smiled. And at that very moment I flushed with a kind of warmth that I had never felt before, at least not that I could remember. Funny that I remembered feeling that way once, back when I was a little dude.

She asked me what I was thinking.

"I don't know," I said. "I was thinking about this police station in Philly and how the water there was—"

"Oh, yeah," she interrupted. "On Haverford Avenue. I grew up around the corner from the station. Yeah, that water was *so* good…"

My Pain Rose

BY TY GRAY-EL

my pain rose like that geyser at Yellowstone

it was old and faithful

yet it leaped and spit and spewed

all over...

my pain rose

it rose like the dust rose

from the World Trade Center

cementing thousands under clouds of anguish...

my pain rose

with prickly thorns protecting its crimson beauty

it stung and hurt and maimed, it tortured

it was old and faithful

like that geyser

hot and humid and cloying...

my pain rose

to greet me at sunrise

issuing forth edicts

from the great State of Depression...

it rose to full mast

like the flag over the Pentagon

the day before September eleventh...

my pain rose early every daybreak

needing no vacation

gray and gloomy like fog

it rose...

my pain was a ventriloquist

using me like a wooden dummy

to herald its preeminence...

it rose from agony's bowels

a deep wound...

it rose like water rises seeking its own level...

it rose and bobbed its ugly head

like empty bottles on a stream...

it rose and lingered and stank

like breath from stale beer...

my pain ached like a decayed bicuspid

throbbing on jangled nerves...

my pain rose

and has risen every morning like clockwork

since the day after you left me... Rose

cupid's curve

BY JIM MORENO

this place on your hip

sacred to me ♀

this place between

bow of belly

and curve of bone ♀

this place that carried

three sons, sacred curve

pilgrim's path,

temple road ♀

Maria D. Dowd

I touch you there

in dawn's faint light ♂

my hand traveling down

your flesh path ♂

fingers tracing artful curve ♂

my life falling down

cupid's song,

my life falling

in order ♂

numinous good fortune

falling like holy rain ♂ ♀

as I touch you softly,

gently in the rosy dawn,

softly…so as not to wake

my love ♂ ♀

I Will Wait for You!

BY WILLIAM B. T. TAYLOR

Meet me on the mountaintop in the midnight hour.

I shall wait for you, amid the peace of my soul I will wait.

Meet me in the quiet space where Spirit lives.

I will wait for you.

In the stillness of the Divine I will wait.

No more cares about the outside dreams, meet me in the
place where we co-create with God.

Where the power lies, no one dies. Where all there is, is love.

You know the place from which you came before you
  were born.

Where you are known as a Goddess.

Where we relate Divinely,

We'll meet in secret, in the Oneness of our Soul.

The place called home,

In the midnight hour,

Meet me there my beloved.

I will wait for you!

If You Were My Herb Garden

BY BEVERLEY EAST

If you were my herb garden

I'd place a crown of cloves upon your head

Where only beautiful dreams reside

Wipe your tears with bay leaves

And nibble on your ear lobes

With scents of sweet basil

That's what I would do if you were my herb garden

I would lick your luscious lips with lavender

Caress your chest with coriander

And soak your soul with sage

Gently wrap your broken heart with ginger root

And make it whole again.

Then I would drum on it with cinnamon sticks

So it pounds to another rhythm

The rhythm of me

Passionate vibrant and kind

Sensuous seductive and wild

That's what I would do if you were my herb garden

I would soothe your stomach with sorrel

And suck on your navel all night

Can I tantalize your thighs with thyme?

And journey to the South

Placing parsley on your pride

Accompanied with mint leaves

Giving hot tea a whole new rhyme

When you are weak

I would put nutmeg in

the crevasses of your knees

Put fennel on your feet

So you never walk away

That's what I would do if you were my herb garden

I would cradle you in a bed of crushed pimentos

Rub you down with rosemary

Sprinkle you with saffron

Infuse your blood with garlic

Spice you up with chilies

And cool you down with chives

My body would be the Saran

That I would wrap around you

Preserving all the essence and beauty you hold

Storing it tight forever

Will you be my herb garden?

So I can play in the wonders of you

And explore the delights of fantasies

If I could tender this garden with love

I promise you honey,

happiness harmony and eternal ecstasy

Jammmm Session

BY MARIA D. DOWD

Dedicated to my beloved husband as a tribute to his genius…

I was drawn to the clangs, the rhythmic sequence that stretched the cracks in the walls like, like life descending, raising the roof with outstretched arms of melodic insanity. Man, the brothas could play. It almost hurt to watch the bangs, the strikes, the chords, the blows, their sweat weighting their dark, single brows lost in a world known only to the souls that created such sounds.

My God, *my* muscles ached wondering how in the world, in *this* world, could such flicks, beats, pounds and brassy

shouts and screams collide with such intensity and such dis-
orderly order of soul and groove, and heart, and vibra-
tion...spirited, unbridled, bare-backed. Those brothas could
play some harmonic madness that got folks up in arms,
flinging arms, skirts and dampness lost in swerves, swings and
more sweat, oh, sweet, sweet sweat—tightly threading the
beating hearts of the swingers with the bad-ass baselines and
nasty notes of these musical marvels.

There was My Baby, a raging flame of passion, a defiant
oneness with the Almighty, palms slicing those skins into
chunks of purrs and cusses and shuns...ahhhh, percussion, percussion so alive it made me tingle, and cry and fall in love all
over again, and again, and again. Jam on, My Sweetness,
jammmm on.

For more information on Maria Dowd's "Journey to Empowerment" and "Journey to a Blissful Life" seminars and speaking engagements; "The Brothas Meet the Sistahs" Tour (meet the contributors of all three books); or other inspirational and home spa gifts, contact Soul Journeys, Inc., P.O. Box 152107, San Diego, CA 92195-2107, 619-229-7766 or 619-229-6156; maria@whatvibes.com; www.warmspirit.org/mariadowd1442; www.whatvibes.com.

Essence bestselling author

Linda Hudson Smith

FIELDS *of* FIRE

A novel

Newly engaged and working in professions
dedicated to saving lives, Stephen Trudeaux and
Darcella Coleman differ on one important decision—
whether to start a family. Then tragedy strikes and
they know it will take much reflection, faith and
soul-searching for their relationship to survive.

*Coming the first week of April,
wherever books are sold.*